Carol Aiko DeShazer Dixon

Return of the Raider presents one survivor's view of the Doolittle Raid against Japan in the early days of World War II after Pearl Harbor. Jacob DeShazer's story is a testament to the grit and determination that saw the U.S. through to victory. *Return of the Raider* is also an unforgettable chronicle of one man's faith during one of the most pivotal times in American history.

—Col. Carroll V. Glines, USAF (Ret.)
Historian, Doolittle's Tokyo Raiders

Jacob DeShazer was brave like a Japanese samurai. He was brave as a prisoner of the Japanese. He never yielded to the guards. After conversion he was braver, enough to love Japanese. As a missionary, he never sought fame or wealth, just the lost. He was kind, patient, and humble, for he was a brave Christian. He was brave enough to make the Japanese commander of the attack on Pearl Harbor one of his best friends. *Return of the Raider* is a story of a person who knew that perfect love drives out all fear.

—Iwao Shimada,
Pastor of the church the DeShazers started in Japan

The wonderful story of hate changed to love was in great demand all over Japan when Jake DeShazer, Florence, and toddler, Paul, arrived in 1949. Although Jake was gone so very much and Florence had the home to care for and Japanese language to study, she was soon involved in teaching Bible Study classes, her special gift. I am happy to endorse a book about this amazing team.

—Marjorie Parsons
Fellow Free Methodist Missionary to Japan

Jake DeShazer lived a life seeking to follow the guidance of the Holy Spirit. So rarely today do we see a similar example of faithfulness in the midst of torture, uncertainty, and our own personal struggles. Goldstein and Dixon tell this story in a way that makes it difficult to put down. We hope to see redemption come out of such difficulty and here we have such a picture. This book will be an inspiration to all who read it.

—Doug Taylor
Seattle Pacific University

Jacob DeShazer, "a man after God's own heart," was respected by Japanese of every degree of social, political, economic, and religious strata, but never changed his purpose, to honor and please God and introduce these acquaintances to Jesus, who came "to seek and to save the lost."

—NORMAN OVERLAND,
FELLOW S.P.C. ALUM AND MISSIONARY TO JAPAN

It was one of the blessings of my life to call Jacob DeShazer my friend. He had a calm, quiet manner that covered the gutsy, inner toughness that helped him stand up to the vicious prison guards of his POW camp. It cannot be denied that God put a Bible in that prison cell. In the 1970's, I had Jake stay in our home (whereas I usually kept guests in hotels). His testimony was riveting and I think his story is packed full of the miraculous graces of God, the transformational power of Scripture, the love God gave Jake for his torturers, and the calling God gave him to return to Japan as a missionary. He frequently told me how, after three-and-a-half years of torturous imprisonment, when he was released his biggest passion was to return to Japan and share Christ with them. *Return of the Raider* captures Jake's testimony and ministry and I am delighted to endorse this wonderful story about my dear old friend.

—DR. PAUL RISSER
FORMER PRESIDENT, THE FOURSQUARE CHURCH

I was a member of the team that located many prisoners of war, including Jacob DeShazer and the other Doolittle raiders. Meeting the three surviving Doolittle Raid flyers at their fifty-ninth reunion in Fresno, California, on March 21, 2001, I was privileged to be reunited with them during the premier of the movie, *Pearl Harbor*. I and my family had the pleasure of a subsequent meeting in Salem, Oregon, with Reverend Jacob DeShazer and his family. Knowing someone as dedicated and spending his lifetime in Japan ministering to the once enemy Japanese was most inspiring.

—DICK HAMADA
MEMBER OF OPERATION MAGPIE AT THE END OF WORLD WAR II

The story of Jacob DeShazer has amazed and inspired people since he and three fellow Doolittle raiders were found alive in a Japanese prison at the end of World War II. With every reason to hate his captors, Jake had discovered a reason to forgive them—the love of Christ. This book by Jake's daughter, Carol, and military historian, Dr. Donald Goldstein, is a long-awaited complete, contemporary biography of the raider who returned, not only to America but to Japan, with a message of hope and healing for the heart.

—DAVID MCCASLAND, CO-PRODUCER, *FROM VENGEANCE TO FORGIVENESS: JAKE DESHAZER'S EXTRAORDINARY JOURNEY*, DAY OF DISCOVERY TELEVISION

For most of my life I have known the name *Jacob DeShazer*. I first heard his story when my grandfather, Dr. Don Falkenberg, published a gospel tract, *I Was a Prisoner of Japan*, which presented the account of Jacob's captivity and imprisonment following the Doolittle Raid. That amazing story recounted how Jacob committed his life to God and His service while in solitary confinement. When Jacob was liberated at war's end, his testimony of God's mercy and saving grace was published in scores of languages with more than thirty million copies in print. One who read that life-changing story was Captain Mitsuo Fuchida, the Japanese commander who led the attack on Pearl Harbor on December 7, 1941. God's love changed the life of that man, and he and Jacob shared God's love with countless people in the following decades.

—JIM FALKENBERG, REACHING SOULS INTERNATIONAL OKLAHOMA CITY, OK

The story of Jake DeSahzer has captivated many of us. Six years and eight months after his first trip to Japan, Jacob, along with Florence and their young son, Paul, arrived in Japan on a different mission. During the DeShazer's career, twenty-three new Free Methodist churches were established throughout Japan. When each group of believers became a worshiping congregation, a church was organized and the DeShazers moved to a new assignment. His was the heart of an evangelist and church planter. We praise the Lord for those in heaven because of his ministry.

—ARTHUR BROWN, EXECUTIVE DIRECTOR, FREE METHODIST WORLD MISSIONS

DONALD M. GOLDSTEIN
CAROL AIKO DESHAZER DIXON

CREATION
HOUSE
A STRANG COMPANY

RETURN OF THE RAIDER by Donald M. Goldstein and
  Carol Aiko DeShazer Dixon
Published by Creation House
A Strang Company
600 Rinehart Road
Lake Mary, Florida 32746
www.strangbookgroup.com

Unless otherwise noted, all Scripture quotations are from the Holy Bible,
New International Version. Copyright © 1973, 1978, 1984, International
Bible Society. Used by permission.

Scripture quotations marked KJV are from the King James Version of the
Bible.

Scripture quotations marked NKJV are from the New King James Version
of the Bible. Copyright © 1979, 1980, 1982 by Thomas Nelson, Inc.,
publishers. Used by permission.

The Scripture quote in Chapter 19 marked MOFFATT is from The Bible: A
New Translation by James Moffatt. Copyright © 1954 by Harper & Row,
New York.

Design Director: Bill Johnson
Cover design: Nathan Morgan

Library of Congress Control Number: 2010929225
International Standard Book Number: 978-1-61638-190-5

First Edition

10 11 12 13 14 — 9 8 7 6 5 4 3 2 1
Printed in the United States of America

CONTENTS

In the last days the mountain of the LORD's temple will be established as chief among the mountains; it will be raised above the hills, and all nations will stream to it. Many peoples will come and say, "Come, let us go up to the mountain of the LORD, to the house of the God of Jacob. He will teach us his ways, so that we may walk in his paths." The law will go out from Zion, the word of the LORD from Jerusalem. He will judge between the nations and will settle disputes for many peoples. They will beat their swords into plowshares and their spears into pruning hooks. Nation will not take up sword against nation, nor will they train for war anymore. Come, O house of Jacob, let us walk in the light of the LORD.

—ISAIAH 2:2–5

PREFACE

THROUGHOUT HISTORY, THERE have been people who have been overlooked despite the fact that they were brilliant, dedicated to duty and a higher purpose, and humble. They did not receive the media accolades or the fame that came with the important work they completed. One such man was Jacob DeShazer, a farm boy from Oregon who grew up during the Great Depression, joined the army, and by the luck of the draw, participated in the famous Doolittle Raid.

After crash landing, he became a prisoner of war for some forty months. During his captivity, he was treated terribly and barely survived. While in solitary confinement he found God and, because of this, was able to survive. He made a vow to God in that prison cell that if he survived he would go back to Japan, not as a warrior but as a missionary. He wanted to introduce to Japan the Christian message of love and forgiveness.

After the war, he enrolled at Seattle Pacific College (now Seattle Pacific University) in Seattle where he met his wife, Florence. Upon the completion of his degree, he returned to Japan and, as he promised, worked there as a missionary for many years. Jacob's testimony influenced the famous leader of the Pearl Harbor attack, Captain Mitsuo Fuchida, to become a Christian. Fuchida would later spread the gospel of Jesus Christ the best that he could in a Buddhist country, which had very little contact with Christianity.

The power of this story is its exploration of the timeless theme of forgiveness, an act that can be contrary to the way we are wired as human beings. It is much easier to seek revenge or to hate than it is to forgive. Jacob DeShazer's story reminds us just how powerful forgiveness, and subsequently, love, can be.

INTRODUCTION

T HE GENESIS OF this book was the drive and determination of Jacob "Jake" DeShazer's family: his wife, Florence, his daughters, Carol Aiko and Ruth, and his sons, John, Mark, and Paul. They lived and breathed their father's life and were there with him from the beginning of his missionary time in Japan to his death in Oregon. They experienced the tough days after the war, being in a country that knew relatively little about Christianity. They lived through the grueling schedule of a missionary and tried their very best to spread the gospel of Jesus Christ. These were difficult times for DeShazer and his family, but while the story is part suffering, it is also about joy and, most importantly, forgiveness, driven from their deep Christian faith.

Return of the Raider is based on Dr. C. Hoyt Watson's book, *The Amazing Story of Sergeant Jacob DeShazer*, which is no longer in print, excerpts from Col. Glines's book, *Four Came Home*, a U.S. Air Force Oral History Interview, several historical videos and audio tapes, and the many letters of Florence DeShazer written to their family over the course of their time in Japan. From Watson's book, we have utilized the extensive interviews that he conducted with Jake during the latter's time as a student at Seattle Pacific College. This, in addition to the Air Force Oral History interview, was an invaluable resource that helped us tell Jake's story in greater detail. Another great resource was Florence's letters. When reading them, one instantly sees the important role she played in this story. In fact, a whole book could be written about Florence's letters. They do a great job of setting the scene, explaining the day-to-day life of the family in Japan, and showing the reader the highs and lows of a missionary family. For future generations of scholars, these letters are available at the University of Pittsburgh Archives Center where copies will be stored.

There have been several attempts to write a book on Jacob DeShazer's life. Some concentrate solely on his prison experience or his early days as a missionary. However, none have sought to give a full account of Jacob's and his family's lives as missionaries in Japan. We believe that this book gives the reader a comprehensive picture of Jacob DeShazer. Moreover, we have received the blessing of the entire family during the completion of this project. Indeed, a special thanks is owed to Carol Aiko DeShazer Dixon, one of Jacob's daughters. She has been the guiding light behind this project and has provided us with the resources and encouragement to undertake this book. Indeed, it was Carol Aiko who kept and preserved her mother's letters and shared them with us. We truly appreciate the help she has given us and we are hopeful that this book will meet the family's expectations.

In 2005, Carol contacted Donald Goldstein who had done a biography with the late Gordon Prange about Mitsuo Fuchida. For three years, Donald Goldstein and Carol Aiko corresponded and finally, in 2008, Goldstein agreed to help her write a book about the life and work of her father. To help him in this endeavor, Goldstein sought the help of two graduate students at the University of Pittsburgh, Kelly McDevitt and Michael Echemendia. Kelly earned her master's degree at the University of Pittsburgh and helped Goldstein sort through the many letters written by Florence DeShazer. Michael, a PhD candidate and former theology student, assisted Goldstein with the research and writing of the book.

Return of the Raider is organized into nineteen chapters that deal with Jacob's early life, his mission over Tokyo, his imprisonment, and his missionary work in Japan. One problem encountered when writing this book occurred regarding the years 1967–1977. The letters were fewer and farther between, with little additional information. This was a period of growth for Jacob's family, but it was also a period of frustration for his ministry, which was not as exciting as in the earlier years. The momentum he had at the beginning had begun to slow. Also, the Japanese people were not as interested in Christianity then as they were in the war's immediate aftermath. The Japanese began to focus their energies on rebuilding and modernizing their country. As such, it became increasingly difficult to get people to attend the Christian meetings and gatherings Jacob held. Despite the lack of significant events during this time period, we found the letters from Florence to be an outstanding depiction of the day-to-day lives, problems, and joys of a missionary and his family.

We would like to thank the Creation House team of Allen Quain, Robert Caggiano, Virginia Maxwell, and Atalie Anderson who worked prudently to bring this book to completion. We are most indebted to the DeShazer family for being so supportive during this process. We are also sure that, if Jake were alive, he would like to dedicate this work to God, Florence, his family, General Jimmy Doolittle and his raiders, and to all the missionaries who preach the gospel of Jesus Christ each day around the world.

Chapter 1

THE FORMATIVE YEARS

Before I formed you in the womb I knew you, before you were born I set you apart.
—Jeremiah 1:5

JACOB DANIEL DESHAZER was born in the small town of Salem, Oregon, on November 15, 1912. He was the seventh of nine children
born to a devout Christian family. Before marrying Hulda, Jacob's
mother, his father brought four children from a previous marriage after
his first wife died. Tragically, Jacob would never have a chance to form a
relationship with his father as he died within two years of Jacob's birth.
Three years passed before Hulda married again. Her new husband was
Mr. Hiram Andrus, a wheat rancher from Madras, Oregon, whom she
met through the aid of the superintendent of the Free Methodist Church
(F.M.C.). Andrus relocated the family to Madras, which was an area
steeped in Indian lore and rich in pioneer history.[1] It was in Madras that
Jacob would spend his formative years.

Madras was sparsely populated with fewer than three hundred people
living in the town.[2] Jake attended elementary school and, in 1927, began
high school. Of all his high school subjects, he was most fond of math-
ematics. This proclivity toward math would later be an asset to Jake in
his military career. Aside from his studies, Jake also enjoyed sports. Although standing only five feet six inches tall, Jake was quite an athlete and
while at Madras High School, he earned letters in football, basketball, and
baseball.

When not in school, the summers for the DeShazer family meant
that Jake, along with his siblings, would be working alongside his father
on the seven hundred acre family farm. Here Jake had a variety of jobs,
which included harvesting wheat and delivering milk. Despite the work,
the children still had the time to swim, fish, and play. Sometimes they all

played church. In the games played by all the children, Ruth, his sister, recalled "Jake liked to play preacher...I don't remember what his sermons were about, but he was getting started on his life's work."[3]

While not rich in material goods, his parents saw that the children had the basic necessities. Another benefit from living on a farm was the presence of animals. The family had a dog named Sport and Jake was the recipient of a pony that his dad bought for twenty-five dollars at an auction at a neighbor's ranch. Jake called the pony Minto and it was Jacob's pride and joy. He truly loved Minto and made sure that she was always treated well. He was very particular about who could ride Minto, and once cried when a group of his friends spanked the horse as they rode. Another family anecdote was the time a visiting girl wanted to ride Jake's horse. The horse's back was sore. Jake protested vehemently and said, "Don't you know that horse is just like my own flesh and blood?"[4]

Minto survived this early mistreatment and lived a long life. However, many years later, the pony had to be shot after it was kicked by another horse and broke its leg in many places. For the family, "It was a sad day... because Jake was a prisoner-of-war and we didn't know whether he was dead or alive." Before shooting the injured pony, Jake's father began to cry and pondered, "I wonder what Jake would say?" His father said that shooting Minto was one of the hardest things he ever had to do.[5]

Being raised in a Christian household meant that Jake was exposed to prayer, the Bible, and church services. But it appeared that Jake had little time for these things, and on Sundays he would dutifully go with his family to the Free Methodist Church in Madras to attend worship services. While Jake would oftentimes stay for the morning preaching service, rather than stay around and meet people after the Benediction, he quickly disappeared.[6] At this point, Christianity was not a major part of Jake's life. Like many young people, he had little time for church. His thoughts were mostly occupied by school, sports, and the family farm. Indeed, for Jake, the Christian faith was something that was experienced only on Sunday rather than the driving force of his life.

At times, his half-sister Helen would ask Jake about his faith. She pressed Jake on whether he believed that Jesus had died on the cross for the sins of the world. Knowing his Roman history, Jake responded by saying that many people were crucified during that time period. While growing up, he believed that Jesus was merely a historical figure, and he did not recognize Jesus' divinity.

His casual relationship with the Christian faith at times manifested itself in Jake's daily actions. To this end, Jake would smoke cigarettes and skip school. He also developed a bad habit of stealing. His parents were quick to address this problem after Jake was caught stealing a man's suitcase. After this incident, his mother and stepfather demanded that Jake apologize for his actions. They then sat down with Jake and prayed with him and for him so that he might ask for God's forgiveness. As Jake recalls, "It was hard to face my fine Christian parents and the neighbors after I had been reported as a thief."[7]

After graduating from high school in 1931, Jake contemplated going to college. This was proving less and less of an option as the country was in the depths of the Great Depression, jobs were scarce, and money was tight. Heretofore, depressions lasted only one to two years. Between 1930 and 1933, 80 percent of the banks in the U.S. failed, which accounted for five thousand banks that were completely wiped out. In 1925, 3 percent of the population was unemployed, but by 1933, 25 percent were unemployed. The high protective tariffs did not stimulate the economy because other countries retaliated against these measures. The grim reality was that people had no money to buy goods, which hurt the average American. Jake's family could barely earn enough money to keep the farm as a result of drought and a poor growing season. Instead of going to college, Jake set out to find work.

At first, Jake stayed close to home and helped with farming, laying hay, and delivering milk. But no job was permanent. He thought about another option, which was to become a diesel mechanic. He looked into the schooling required to become a mechanic, but his one-dollar-a-day wage would not allow him to pay the fifty dollars required to attend the school. After two years of working jobs exclusively in Madras, Jake believed that he had to expand his horizons. He believed there would be more opportunities if he looked beyond Madras. This took him first to California.

In California, Jake took any odd job he could find. He cut branches off peach trees, and even picked cotton and potatoes. The tasks were menial and labor-intensive. Later in life, he half-jokingly remembered, "Boy, those sacks were heavy and the work was hard."[8] Never one to do things the easy way, Jake wound up in the hospital with a broken leg after a horse had fallen on him. After being in the hospital, he was able to find employment as a cattle and sheep tender on a small ranch on the California-Nevada border.

Jake greatly enjoyed this type of work. For two years he was able to live outdoors like a cowboy as he kept watch over three to four thousand sheep. He even cooked his meals over an open campfire. The job required a healthy constitution, as Jake would spend most his time outdoors. He lived in the horse's saddle as he traveled with sheep and cattle to the beautiful California mountains in the spring and summer, then on to the flat Nevada desert in the winter. Reminiscing to his friends and family about this experience, Jake commented that he "enjoyed going to the mountains in the summertime and back to the deserts of Nevada in the winter."[9]

Since there was little opportunity to spend money in the Nevada desert or the California mountains, at the end of two years Jake had saved up one thousand dollars. To Jake, one thousand dollars was an awful lot of money. With this money, Jake decided to try his hand at business. Being a product of the independent West, Jake wanted to be self-reliant. He did not want to work for anyone, but preferred the idea of being his own boss. Jake's business idea involved raising turkeys. Having spent a considerable amount of time growing up around turkeys, Jake believed that he could raise these creatures and make a profit for himself. With this idea in mind, Jake moved to Butte Falls, Oregon, where he bought a farm and then purchased five hundred young turkeys.

The plan was to raise the turkeys to sell them at Thanksgiving. In Jake's mind, he would fatten the birds up right in time for the holiday. To this end, he cared for the birds day and night. He watched them closely and spared no expense to ensure that the birds had sufficient food, shelter, and personal care.

However, as with most business ventures, there were risks involved. Jake assumed that the price of turkey meat would stay steady or rise before Thanksgiving. However, as luck would have it, the price of turkey meat dropped from twenty-two cents a pound to thirteen or fourteen in the days leading up to Thanksgiving. When all the birds were sold, Jacob made no profit and did not have enough money to continue his business. In fact, Jake was flat broke. Once again, Jacob was confronted with the questions of where to go and what to do. He was a twenty-seven-year-old bachelor with no money and few job prospects, so Jake decided the military might be the answer.

Chapter 2

ARMY TRAINING

From heaven he made you hear his voice to disci-
pline you. On earth he showed you his great fire,
and you heard his words from out of the fire.
—Deuteronomy 4:36

ON FEBRUARY 26, 1940, more than a year and a half before the bombing of Pearl Harbor, Jake joined the army Air Corps at Fort McDowell in California. While the U.S. was not directly involved at the time, the world was in turmoil. Hitler's Germany was taking territory and spreading destruction and upheaval across Europe. Meanwhile, Japan was establishing itself as a major power in Asia as it continued to extend its influence in the Pacific.

Jacob had a fascination with airplanes and always wanted to be a pilot. He believed being a pilot would be a great way to serve his country. As a child, his sister Ruth recalled, "Jake was about six the first time we ever saw an airplane. I remember him yelling, 'It's mine! It's mine! Mom, it's mine!' He was so insistent that Mother said, 'Sure, Jakie, it's yours. You can have it.'"

However, his dream of becoming a pilot was short-lived. At twenty-seven, he was too old by military standards to begin pilot's training. Instead, the military sent him to the Boeing School of Aeronautics in Oakland, California, to train him to become an airplane mechanic. A few years earlier, Jake had considered pursuing a similar career in the private sector, but was unable to due to lack of funds. Now with the U.S. military paying the bill for his training, Jake believed he would become a mechanic and later could start his own business.

When his training was complete, he was stationed at McCord Field near Tacoma, Washington. At McCord, Jake worked as a mechanic on the North American B-25 Mitchell bomber. Although he was forced to give up his dream of being a pilot, he was able to fly when the military began looking for bombardiers. The bombardier's main duty was to assist the pilot and navigator to ensure that a bomb hits the target. This excited Jake and he applied and was accepted to bombardier school.

Being a bombardier came easy to Jake. He had plenty of practice shooting at moving targets from when he was growing up in Madras. Indeed, Jake and his brother used to shoot jackrabbits while on horseback or from a Model T Ford. Jake said, "We didn't think that we were very good if we could not get them while they were running. So sitting in the B-25 and just getting those crosshairs on that target down there at twenty thousand feet seemed like a pretty easy thing to me."[10]

Jake settled into the mundane routine of military life. According to Jake, "I had been living the kind of life that most of the enlisted men lived. I would associate with certain fellows and we would go to dances and drinking places to pass away our spare time. I feel ashamed of the events that took place in my life during those years. There is really no reason why anyone should want to live such a life. It does not lead to happiness."[11]

On December 7, 1941, the Japanese attacked Pearl Harbor. After the bombing, Jake was transferred from Camp Pendleton to an air base in Columbia, South Carolina. Jake was on kitchen police (better known as "KP") duty when he first heard of the Japanese surprise attack. Upon hearing the news, Jake became enraged and shouted that the Japanese were going to pay for the attack. Jake thought the Japanese were crazy for doing something so deliberate.

The Japanese attack succeeded in catching the U.S. by surprise and hurting U.S. morale. Indeed, after the Pearl Harbor attack, U.S. morale was at an all-time low. In the U.S., the attack had the effect of igniting a fervent hatred against the Japanese almost overnight. A few weeks after the attack, on February 19, 1942, President Roosevelt issued Executive Order 9066, which oversaw the internment of more than one hundred thousand persons of Japanese descent, including many U.S. citizens, in military camps. Persons of Japanese ancestry were also banned from entering the entire Pacific coast area, including California, Oregon, and Washington.

During the first few months of World War II, after their successful attack on Pearl Harbor, the Japanese added to their victory by sinking the British battleships *Prince of Wales* and *Repulse*. The Japanese juggernaut swept down through French Indo-China, across Thailand, and marched through Malaya, Burma, and Ceylon to capture what once had been the impregnable fortress of Singapore. They had taken the Philippines and lost no time in adding Sumatra, Java, Borneo, and the Celebes to the imperial reign of Hirohito. They occupied New Britain, New Ireland, New Hebrides, and small groups of islands opposite the Dutch East Indies. When they took the Solomon Islands, only New Guinea stood between them and their projected conquest of Australia. Before their final drive, they paused to consolidate and regroup.

Their tactics were relatively simple. As they drove south against token opposition, they built airfields along the way to extend the attacking range for their aircraft. In the early days, when the Japanese were not making mistakes, they took their objectives with high precision and little loss of life. There were no massive attacks with men marching shoulder to shoulder, no frontal assaults as in World War I. Instead, the Allies found themselves fighting an invisible enemy that hid from retreating Allied columns, blocked roads, staged ambushes, and when the battle got too hot, disappeared into the jungle. It was the simplicity of their tactics, more than anything else, which made them a formidable foe. They were more than a match for an unprepared enemy. As they succeeded, the myth of their invincibility was perpetuated by their elaborate propaganda machine and by the many war correspondents who wrote about their victories.

In order to boost American morale, President Franklin Roosevelt asked his Joint Chiefs to come up with a plan to attack the Japanese mainland. He was intent on responding to blatant Japanese aggression. The response needed to be strong and it had to hurt Japanese morale. But how to respond? The U.S. had lost bases in the Pacific and the naval fleet was damaged, but luckily the aircraft carriers remained intact. Enter James "Jimmy" Doolittle, an ace from World War I who came up with a daring plan that involved taking the fight to the Japanese mainland.

The decision to attack Japan was important because the Japanese believed their homeland was inviolable and divinely protected by the gods. Doolittle wanted to shatter this notion and sow seeds of doubt among the Japanese people. After careful planning, it was determined that only military targets would be attacked. In order to do this, he needed a few brave volunteers.

While working on an airplane in a hangar one day, Jake received an order to report directly to the captain. Why, he wondered. What had he done to warrant this? He would find out in short order. Upon arrival, Jake found about twenty other men in the room with him. The captain began telling them of a dangerous mission that was being planned and that some of them would not make it back. He proceeded to ask the men if they would like to volunteer for such a mission. Everyone enthusiastically agreed to go. In his mind, Jake could not see how he could say no. He realized this was a real opportunity for adventure and excitement!

All of the volunteers needed to be trained to take part in this "dangerous mission." The training began in Columbia, South Carolina, where they all met a short man by the name of Lieutenant Colonel James Doolittle, who was the mission architect and commander. Doolittle impressed Jake from the beginning, walking up to him, talking to him, and knowing his name. After the encounter, Jake recalled, "He's my leader. He's the fellow for the job, whatever it is."[12]

One week after the meeting in the captain's office, nearly 120 volunteers made their way to Eglin Field in the Florida panhandle. The 120 volunteers were divided into twenty-four crews with each having a pilot, copilot, navigator, bombardier, and a gunner/engineer. At Eglin, they trained by going out on bombing missions. Throughout the training, low-level flying and short take-offs were the most practiced maneuvers.

Jake continued his training as an airplane mechanic and bombardier. His pilot, Lieutenant William Farrow, became adept at low flying. Often, the crew would fly so low across the fields that they almost hit fences.[13]

Once Doolittle retuned from a visit to Washington, the training picked up. The planes were loaded with heavy practice bombs and the pilots were tasked with getting the planes off the ground despite short runway distances of five hundred to seven hundred feet.[14] When the order came for the crew to leave Florida and travel to San Francisco, there was a palpable excitement in the air. Although they had no idea of the mission they would be asked to do, rumors abounded. Some thought that the mission would take them to Japan. Others believed the mission to be in Europe. The men had an inkling that the mission involved a carrier, but whether it would be in Europe or Japan, no one knew.

Ever eager to practice their new maneuvers, the crew turned the flight to San Francisco into one long practice flight. Jake's pilot began to get comfortable with flying the plane at low altitudes. As Jake notes, "When we got to Texas and New Mexico, we could see the cattle in the fields. Our pilots would fly low in order to frighten the animals. It was great sport to see them put their tails in the air and run for all they were worth. We thought that was lots of fun and were glad to be in the army and see something exciting."[15]

Before the trip to California, they had to turn their planes over to civilian technicians for final inspections, which did not bode well with them, and especially not with Jake, a trained military mechanic. He had volunteered for this special, dangerous mission. When the civilian technicians returned the planes, Jake and his buddies checked them out to be sure that they were not tampered with and were still in good shape.

With the planes safely aboard the *U.S.S. Hornet*, the men waited on the ship still in the dark about their impending mission. They passed their time reading, drinking, and playing cards. The night prior to departure, they were given free leave. The crew spent their time dancing the night away at a local establishment. They spent seventeen days on board the *Hornet* before the mission began. A corporal at the time, Jake was the lowest ranking man of his crew. He was called to perform guard duty on numerous occasions. While on guard duty, Jake had plenty of time to think about the special mission he was a part of and whether he would survive.[16] His mind began to race as he thought in earnest about what the mission entailed. When not on guard duty, or when the crew was not working on their aircraft, they had plenty of free time. It was all a waiting game. The soldiers tried their best to keep boredom at bay. It was during this time that Jake wrote his mother, "Don't worry about me, mother. I am in no danger."[17]

On April 1, 1942, all sixteen B-25 bombers were placed on the flight deck of the *U.S.S. Hornet*. Jake's plane was the last one. It was anchored to the flight deck with a portion of the plane's tail hanging over the stern of the carrier.[18] The next day, the *Hornet* left dock and sailed beneath the Golden Gate Bridge. As the boat steamed westward, other ships joined the convoy until the entire task force was completed with a total of twelve ships: the aircraft carrier *Hornet*, another carrier, the *Enterprise*, two cruisers, two tankers, and six destroyers.[19]

After their first hour underway, the ship's announcement system rang out calling every man to attention. In the next few minutes, the men received partial details of their mission. It was to be a daring expedition— bombing Japan! The ships would not be stopping at any other port during their journey. They were to travel with haste to Japan.

When they heard about the mission to attack Japan, the two thousand sailors and airmen of the *Hornet* began cheering. This was turning out to be a grand adventure. The idea of attacking the enemy in his own backyard thrilled them. They thought their attack on Japan would help bring a stop to Japanese aggression in the Pacific and avenge those who died at Pearl Harbor. Jake experienced this charged environment and reflected, "I sensed a fighting spirit among these men. We did not have to have speeches to point out what was wrong with Japan. Every person seemed to know that Japan was an outlaw and would have to be forced to surrender. The Japanese were taking things that didn't belong to them. They had started the war. These American men were ready to fight against such unrighteousness."[20]

The men believed they were on a crusade in order to right wrong and bring about the end of a war. Jake began to reflect on the crew that would help him in his mission. When describing the crew, Jake said modestly, "We found out that we were the least trained of any of the crews of the B-25s."[21] There was the pilot of Jake's plane, Lieutenant William Farrow, a towering six-foot six-inch tall individual from South Carolina. Next, there was the Texan copilot, Lieutenant Robert Hite, the navigator, Lieutenant George Barr from New York, and the tailgunner, Sergeant Harold Spatz, from Kansas.[22] These men had already been through a great deal of training together. However, before their mission, they had little idea of just how well acquainted they would become with each other.

After all the excitement, the reality began to set in for Jake. While on guard duty the first night after setting off from San Francisco, Jake began to have doubts. Thoughts of mortality and the afterlife crept into Jake's mind as the *Hornet* traveled west toward Japan. He said, "I began to wonder how many more days I was to spend in this world. Maybe I wasn't so fortunate after all to get to go on this trip. I tried to comfort myself with statistics, which I could recall. I reminded myself that more than fifty thousand Americans had been killed in the First World War. I shuddered to think where I would go if I was to die."[23]

While these thoughts assailed Jake when his mind was free to wander at night, during the day things were much different. Jake filled his time training, playing cards with the men, and observing the seals and birds that followed the ship. Of particular interest to Jake was an albatross. Jake noted that, "The albatross followed us, flying on tireless wings. I watched their graceful flying each day. It seemed strange that they could keep up to the aircraft carrier and never appear to move their wings. These strange birds didn't have to go to school to learn how to fly. They were shown the way to fly by their Creator."[24]

The time Jake spent alone proved to be a time of introspection and searching. Looking out on the horizon with nothing but ocean as far as the eye could see he recalled, "I felt a longing for something which is hard to describe. I did not know what that longing was at that time. The Creator was certainly trying to manifest Himself to me by this great display of His creation. Job 12:9 tells us, 'Who knoweth not in all these that the hand of the LORD hath wrought this?' (KJV). I longed for fellowship with this Creator. I did not know at that time how God would gladly fellowship with His creation. I did not realize that God would gladly fellowship with me, if I would meet the conditions written in the Bible."[25]

The thoughts Jake was having at this time were indeed a prelude to his conversion, which he would experience in a most unlikely place. Questions about God and the afterlife were secondary to Jake at this time in his life. Growing up in a Christian household laid the foundation for his faith. His parents imparted to him the central importance of the Bible, of prayer, and of a personal relationship with Jesus. However, Jake had yet to make the faith of his parents his own. As with most young people, Jake believed himself to be self-reliant. After all, he was a product of the rugged and individualistic West. He had worked on farms, braved the mountains of California, and survived the deserts of Nevada. He knew hard work, he was familiar with sacrifice, and he never asked for help. What Jake did not realize was that there were heavenly forces at work in his life that he was slowly beginning to understand. However, a fuller understanding of them would have to wait. To this end, Jake did not go out of his way to attend church services while on the *Hornet*. On April 5, Easter Sunday, a service was held for the men. While many men attended the service, Jake did not.[26]

Chapter 3

THE MISSION

For a long time now—to this very day—you have
not deserted your brothers but have carried out
the mission the LORD your God gave you.

—Joshua 22:3

THE CREW OF the *Hornet* continued to speculate about what their
mission would be. During the card and craps games, idle conversation wandered over a host of different scenarios. They knew
they were on a mission to bomb Japan, but details were scarce about what
that actually meant. On Friday, April 17, the commander of the task force
ended the guessing game. He announced, "This task force has been directed to proceed to a position four hundred miles east of Japan. The
army bombers will be launched from the *U.S.S. Hornet*. They will bomb
Tokyo."[27]

The last sentence reverberated in the men's ears. They were going to
bomb Tokyo! What a daring move. The men believed that this would show
the Japanese that the Americans were not a paper tiger. They, after all, had
attacked the U.S. The U.S. did not want to take part in the war, but the
Japanese violated the rules by perpetrating an unprovoked attack, killing and wounding thousands of U.S. military personnel and civilians. For
this perceived cowardly act, Jake and the men aboard the *Hornet* believed
that Japan should be punished because what they did was tantamount to
murder in their minds. Some of the men started singing their own version
of a song from *Snow White*, "Hi Ho, Hi Ho, it's off to Tokyo we go! We'll
bomb and blast, and come back fast."[28]

The jovial mood soon began to change as the singing died down. The
men became reflective and everywhere on the ship there was an unmistakable tension. Yes, they were going to bomb Japan. Yes, they were going
to avenge the thousands who had died at Pearl Harbor. And yes, they

might not come back alive. But one question arose in the minds of the crew, "How close to Tokyo can we get without being spotted?"[29] Surely they could not get too close or else the Japanese would know they were coming. Another burning question was that they did not know when the order to depart would be given. These thoughts greatly increased the anxiety of the men as they waited for the call to take off. [30]

As the mission was quickly approaching, the men, instead of playing cards, began to pour over maps of Japan. Now there was much less idle conversation and no laughter could be heard. When it came time for the men to turn in, many went to sleep with their clothes on.[31]

According to historical documents, it is known that the original plan was for the planes to take off from the *Hornet* late Saturday evening, April 18. This would allow the bombers to conduct their bombing runs on Sunday morning. Next, they would head northwest toward China so that they could land there and refuel. There were two events that altered the plan. First, a lookout for the *Hornet* spotted two Japanese surface craft. It was quite possible that those craft were part of a patrol unit. The call to stations alarm was sounded at 3:15 in the morning on Saturday, April 18. The men hurried out of bed and ran to their battle stations.[32] Fortunately for the *Hornet* and Doolittle's raiders, the Japanese did not see them. The night provided good cover, which made the ships difficult to see. At that time, the task force was nine hundred miles east of Japan. The hope was to approach until the task force was approximately four hundred miles from Japan before the planes were launched.[33]

The second scare happened shortly after dawn when one fishing boat and two Japanese destroyers were sighted. Feeling as though the ships had seen the task force, the Admiral, William "Bull" Halsey, believed their element of surprise had been compromised. He believed the destroyers had seen the U.S. ships and were in the process of radioing that information ahead to the Japanese imperial command.[34]

Immediately, one of Halsey's cruisers opened fire on the fishing boat. Although the seas were rough that morning, the U.S. cruiser made quick work of the fishing boat as it was sent to the bottom of the ocean. One U.S. cruiser quickly left the convoy to engage the Japanese destroyers. Some time passed before the U.S. cruiser radioed in that it had successfully sunk the Japanese ships.[35]

A split-second decision had to be made: should they hold the attack and try to get closer to Japan? Or should they launch the attack immediately? The commander opted for the latter. An announcement came over the *Hornet's* loudspeakers telling the men that all aircraft should be prepared for immediate departure. The men were told, "Army personnel, man your airplanes and take off immediately! If you can't get your motor started, we'll have to shove them off into the ocean."[36] The order was relayed to the other ships in the task force, "*Hornet* preparing to launch bombers for attack on Tokyo."[37]

Men ran to their stations. Every movement was methodical. The intense training had paid off and each person knew what to do in order to get the bombers airborne. As Jake was crawling into the back of his plane, another sergeant shouted to him, "We just got one chance in a thousand of making it."[38] Making it? Did the sergeant mean making the take off, which the planes had to do in four hundred fifty feet rather than the seven hundred feet the men had been practicing? Or did he mean making it back alive? No matter, there was little time for this type of thinking. Despite the fear, the men felt a sense of excitement coursing through their veins. This was it! This was the moment that they all had been training for! Now came the first challenge, getting the planes off the ship.

The carrier was dipping up and down with the waves and there was a bit of fog. Every person on the *Hornet* was anxious to see how the planes would get airborne. All eyes were fixed on Colonel Doolittle's bomber. It only had four hundred fifty feet, a little more half the distance they had trained for. This seemed like an impossible feat. The takeoff process was like a choreographed dance on the water. As the carrier pitched over each swell, the deckhands had to time the rise and fall of the flight deck over each wave. When the timing was right, the deckhand would drop his flag, the pilot released the plane's brakes, and the plane would begin its takeoff roll downhill gathering speed while riding along the deck, until it took off.

It helped that Doolittle was a skilled pilot. With his engines straining at full throttle, he released the brakes and was sent speeding down the carrier deck. When the *Hornet's* bow dipped, the airplane took to the air. At first sight, it looked like the plane had crashed into the ocean, but soon it began to rise in altitude and leveled off. Doolittle then circled over the *Hornet* as a farewell salute, to which the men erupt in cheers.[39] Their nervousness gone, the deck crew prepared to launch the other fifteen planes. One by one they all took off from the carrier, an amazing achievement in its own right.

When it came time for Jake's plane, number sixteen out of sixteen, affectionately named the *Bat Out of Hell*, there was some trouble. Due to the crowded conditions on the carrier, number sixteen was put on the edge of the deck at the stern, with the plane's tail literally hovering over the open ocean. Before the plane was ready to take off, a gust of wind blew pushing the nose of the plane up. To those on deck, it looked like the plane was about to do a backflip into the ocean.

Quick thinking sailors tied ropes to the nose of the plane in an effort to stabilize it. The ropes proved too feeble to hold the plane. More sailors rushed over to the plane and more ropes were attached to the nose. Jake himself even got out of the plane to assist. Through sheer strength and determination, the men were able to hold the plane on the deck. In the commotion, one sailor backed into the propeller of the airplane. With the engines already running, the sailor's arm was completely severed. Jake called another sailor to help the injured man because he knew that he would be directly in the path of the wheel if he remained where he was. Jake helped carry the man to the other side of the deck so that the plane could get ready to take off.[40] Despite the man's pain, he looked at Jake and told him, "Give them hell for me."[41]

Jake got back into the plane with his crew. While they were in line to take off, Jake noticed a small hole about one foot in diameter located in the nose of the gun mount. Jake was amazed that nobody had noticed this. The next question that popped into his mind was how the hole got there! It must have occurred when Jake's plane hit the plane directly in front of it. Jake thought about telling the pilot, however his sense of duty got the best of him. He distinctly remembered that if there were any problems with the plane, it would not go on the mission and would be pushed overboard. So Jake kept quiet and said nothing. He wanted to fly the mission and knew that his crew did, too. He buckled himself in and thought, "Take a chance on it."[42]

The pilot gave the thumbs up to the deckhand. With the engines revved to full throttle, the breaks were released and the *Bat Out of Hell* careened down the deck and took off perfectly. With all the planes airborne, Jake noticed that the *Hornet* had already changed its course. While its mission was now complete, the Doolittle raiders were just starting theirs.

Once they were in flight, Jake decided to tell Lieutenant Farrow, "We've got a hole in this thing about a foot in diameter."[43] After taking a look at the damage, they decided to stuff the hole with their coats, but

the wind just kept blowing them back in, so they decided to fly on anyway. What choice did they have? They were airborne and heading toward
Japan. What the crew did realize was that this hole would make it hard for
them keep up with the rest of the bombers. Indeed, the *Bat* was unable to
hold formation. The commander of one of the other planes, Colonel John
Hilger, reported that he lost sight of Lieutenant Farrow's plane soon after
takeoff.[44] The hole greatly reduced the aerodynamic integrity of the B-25,
which caused the plane to burn fuel at a higher rate.[45] The crew realized
that this would be an issue after they had made their bombing run. They
might not have enough fuel to reach China. The men banished these dark
thoughts and focused on the mission at hand.

The *Bat* left the *Hornet* at approximately 9:20 a.m. For the next thirteen hours, the plane skimmed the ocean at one hundred feet in order
to avoid radar detection. At one point they were so low that a propeller
blade tipped a wave. After that they decided to fly a little higher, but always stayed low because "they didn't know whether they [Japan] had good
radar or not."[46] The entire flight lasted about thirteen hours with the plane
reaching Japan around 1:00 p.m.

As they approached Japan, mountains appeared in front of them. To
safely get over the mountains, the plane had to climb to an altitude of
seven thousand feet. The crew kept an eye out. Soon, one of the crewmembers saw people below. Jake looked out the window. The Japanese
were surprised to see a plane and mistakenly took it to be Japanese. At
one point, Jake noticed an old man walking along a mountain trail with a
cane. Hearing the plane, he turned around to observe it then threw himself on the ground as the plane sped by him.[47]

Once the mountains were cleared, they stayed hidden in the clouds
until they reached their target. Instead of Tokyo, Jake's plane had been assigned to Nagoya, a town about three hundred miles south of the capital.
The weather that day was clear with the sun shining. As they approached
the city, the pilot told Jake to "get set to drop the bombs at five hundred feet. There is the first target."[48] The pilot's message shook Jake. Five
hundred feet? They had been practicing at three times that altitude. According to Jake, "I had never gone down to five hundred feet before, so I
was kinda surprised." The pilot then asked him, "See that gasoline tank?"
It was right near a tower in Nagoya. Jake continued, "We flew right over it,
and boy, I had that thing [the makeshift bombsight] set for five hundred.
There wasn't any bombsight. It was just a thing they had made, but it was

calibrated so that five hundred feet was on there. I hit the switch, and my pilot went around and turned."[49]

The crew then proceeded to their next targets, an aircraft factory and another gasoline storage facility. Jake described the situation as follows:

> We were making a complete turn, and I smelled smoke. I wanted to see how an oil refinery looked when it was on fire. To the left of us, I saw where the first bombs had dropped. There was fire all over the tank, but it had not blown up yet. What I smelled, however, was the powder from the anti-aircraft shells that were being shot at us instead of the bombs I had dropped. I had noticed a little black smoke cloud right in front of us, and evidently the hole in the nose of our airplane allowed the smoke to come inside.
>
> We went over a big factory-looking building and dropped the last incendiary. We skimmed along down a valley on our way out to the ocean. I was getting ready to shoot. There is something about being shot at that makes you want to shoot back. I had read in the newspapers one time about a German aviator shooting at French people, and I thought it was a mean thing to do. I made up my mind while on the *Hornet* that I would not shoot at civilians. But after they shot at us, I changed my mind.
>
> I saw a man standing in a fishing boat, waving as we came along. He thought that we were Japanese. I thought that I would show him that we weren't. I shot a few shots near him, and the poor fellow stopped waving. I wasn't a very good shot, however, and therefore no harm was done.
>
> We flew along the coast of Japan intending to fly on the Thirteenth Parallel to Choo Chow Lishui, in China. We saw several of the other B-25's, but did not follow any of them. When night came, we saw dimly the coastline of China, but the fog was so

thick we could not tell what part of China we were approaching.

Our navigator, Lieutenant Barr, was doing lots of paper work. He said we should be over Choo Chow Lishui. The pilot circled, calling on the radio all the time. No answer came back. The fog cleared off a little. We could see a town below but no airfield.

In the tanks we had gasoline enough for only one hour. We had to do something and Lieutenant Farrow was anxious to save the B-25. It was a good old gas burner. With a hole in the nose it had already stayed in the air for more than thirteen hours. By flying beyond Japanese-held territory, we could get to Keyon in Free China, where more gasoline was stored. We might be able to see the airfield or get a response from the Chinese radio operator.

After we had flown for another hour, we saw a town. Our gasoline was nearly gone. We circled the town, calling and looking for lights from an airfield, but to no avail. Finally, Lieutenant Farrow said, "We gotta jump." It was 11:40 p.m. The airplane was at an altitude of three thousand feet. I watched Lieutenant Barr go first. Then I jumped.

It wasn't exactly a jump. I put my legs out and the wind knocked them against the fuselage of the airplane so hard that I had to push against the door-frame in order to get out of the opening on the lower side of the fuselage. I gave a shove and then watched the plane go over my head. I lost my hat as the wind was shrieking over me. When the plane had gone beyond me, I pulled the ripcord and was given a hard but welcome jerk immediately when the parachute opened. I watched the light go out of sight from the opening in the fuselage of the plane. Soon the sound of the motors died out. Everywhere I looked, it was dark. The fog was thick around me, and I felt a strange sensation of loneliness.

I had no way of knowing that I was coming down since I could not see the ground and there was no sensation of wind since the parachute had opened. I began to wonder if I would have to sit up there all night. The place where I landed was the final resting grounds of a Chinese man. I threw my arms around that mound of dirt and gave it a big hug. I was glad to be back on the ground, even if it was a good long way from the U.S.A.

I saw several mounds of dirt and noticed that I was on a knoll. Then I realized it was a Chinese grave-yard. All around were rice fields, which were under water at that time of year. I found out later that at the very time I was coming down in the parachute, my mother was awakened from her sleep and was praying for me.[50]

Indeed, many miles away, Jake's mother, Hulda Andrus, suddenly awoke the very night that her son parachuted out of the *Bat*. She described the experience, "I awakened suddenly one night with a strange feeling, like being dropped down, down, down through the air. Oh, the terrible burden that weighted my soul! I prayed and cried out to God in my distress. Suddenly, the burden was gone, and I drifted off into an untroubled sleep, something unusual for me. Comparing the time here with the time in occupied China, it was just the time when Jacob had had to parachute from his falling plane. How I praise the Lord now, but of course I didn't realize or know what was taking place so far away. When we heard in the war news that our airmen had been over Tokyo dropping bombs, little did I realize that my own precious boy was in the crew of one of the planes."[51]

As Jake parachuted into the unknown, another thought occurred to him. He wondered what would happen if he died. Where would his soul go? Jake's question recalls a statement made by the apostle Thomas in the Gospel of John. Thomas asks Jesus, "Lord, we don't know where you are going, so how can we know the way?"[52] Jake, like Thomas, was confused about where his life was going and what he should do to change it. Indeed, according to Jake, "I was worried about dying the way I was. I was immoral and wasn't living right, and I didn't know whether or not I was going to hell or what was going to happen."[53] For the moment, circumstances forced Jake to stop thinking about this question. He needed to figure out where he was, where his crew was, and devise a plan to get home.

Chapter 4

Captivity

"I will be found by you," declares the Lord,
"and will bring you back from captivity."
—*Jeremiah 29:14*

Upon landing, Jake experienced a sharp pain in his chest. He realized that he must have broken a few ribs when he hit the Chinese grave.[54] Although in some pain, he was able to cut himself free from the parachute and move about. At first, he cautiously wandered around the graveyard. It was located atop a hill and the land was surrounded by water. Then he shot his pistol into the air several times, but he got no response from his crew.[55] Jake had to confront the terrible thought that he might be alone. Having no way to find out what happened to his crew, he tried to press on in the dark. However, the pouring rain and slippery mud made for slow going. Walking about for a few minutes, Jake came across a small brick building that had been used as a shrine by the Chinese. Even though it was very small, he believed that if he cleared it out, he could use it as a shelter. To that end, "I shoved the irons out of the way where they burn their incense, and got out of the rain." He intended only to rest for a few minutes, but the exhaustion caught up with him. He slept until morning and with the daylight was able to get a better idea of his surroundings. Jake began walking westward.[56]

After walking for a few hours, Jake came upon a road with some people. Jake said, "It looked awful strange, you know? The people were sort of different there. Looked like they weren't very intelligent people right in the area...It must have gotten flooded every year, as it was under a lot of water. I couldn't get anything out of the people there. Was this area Japanese-occupied or free China?"[57]

He continued walking until he came across a store. Jake wandered in and tried to write down a few words to communicate with the Chinese shopkeeper. The shopkeeper just shook his head in confusion. Frustrated, Jake left the road and pressed on. After a time, he came across a main road and a telephone line. This gave Jake some hope as he could use the phone to get help. Walking along the road exposed Jake to a level of poverty and misery he had not known existed in the world. As Jake recalled, "I could see inside their mud houses. Chickens, pigs, and children wading around together in filthy mud inside the house. The people had heads about the size of a four year old child in America. The skin on their faces was wrinkled and old looking. I didn't expect to find out much from them. I didn't care to ask them for anything to eat although I was getting very hungry."[58]

As he made his way along the highway, he came upon a camp that contained military personnel. Jake did not just want to walk into a Japanese camp, so he retraced his steps and came across a house that was riddled with bullets. Nearby, there were some young soldiers playing with children. Jake asked them China or Japan? One replied "China," which he then wrote on a piece of paper. Jake replied "America." He was nervous. He did not know whether they were being truthful. One turned around and left, making Jake even more uncertain. Jake decided it would be in his best interest to keep going, but he was called back by one of the men. Jake offered him cigarettes and they tried to carry on a conversation, but all he said was "China."[59] This was getting Jake nowhere and his fear intensified. He had a .45 pistol with seven bullets in the chamber to protect himself. However, if more people came, Jake knew that he would be easily outnumbered and outgunned.

The man he had been speaking with beckoned Jake to come into a shed to sit. Jake recalled, "I don't know how he got me into that shed, but we got into that shed and I couldn't see around, and pretty soon, around on the side that was open came eight or ten fellows with guns." Jake put his hand on his pistol, but did not draw it. He began to yell to the soldiers, "China or Japan?" They yelled back "China." Not wanting to shoot Chinese soldiers, Jake let them come into the shed.[60]

The soldiers came into the shed. They tried to act friendly with Jake by shaking his hand, patting him on the back, and smiling at him. The soldiers led Jake out of the shed and back on the main road. As they walked, Jake felt the tip of a bayonet against his back. He instinctively went to reach his pistol, when one of the soldiers who spoke some English said, "We think you better let us have your gun."[61] Jake, finding himself surrounded by soldiers in a foreign country, had no choice but to turn over the gun.

When they reached the camp, Jake was given some yokan, a mashed-up sweet bean with sugar and mixed with something like pancake dough. He was hungry, as he hadn't eaten for at least twenty-four hours. The men then asked how Jake got there. Jake answered "I don't know" to every question he was asked.

A short time later, his worst fears came true. The men told him he was a prisoner of the imperial Japanese army. "Aren't you afraid?" asked the interpreter. Jake replied, "What should I be afraid of?" Aside from his calm outside demeanor, Jake was worried. He was not sure if the Japanese knew he was an airman. He thought that it had been a good idea to destroy his parachute upon landing, as Doolittle had ordered, keeping only a small section of it to keep his head dry.[62]

He was later taken to another town. Being disoriented, he had no idea where he was going or what his fate would be. Here, Jake learned that four of his crewmates had also been captured. They saw each other the next morning as they were photographed in front of a building.[63] This was not the happy reunion that they intended to have.

Chapter 5

TRIAL AND VERDICT

Whenever you are arrested and brought to trial, do not worry
beforehand about what to say. Just say whatever is given you
at the time, for it is not you speaking, but the Holy Spirit.
—*Mark 13:11*

JAKE AND THE crew were weary. They had been awake for almost an
entire day. The next morning, they found little rest as the Japanese
loaded them up into a transport plane and flew them to another city.
When they arrived, the prisoners were taken off the plane and placed in a
makeshift prison. The cells were made of wooden bars and the room was
bare with the exception of a small wooden latrine.[64]

Later that evening, Jake was brought into a room where a group of
Japanese officers began to question him. He described the experience:

> One of the officers, using lots of slang, said that I
> had better talk. He said that these were mean people,
> and they would torture me until I did talk. I was still
> blindfolded as I had been most of the time for more
> than twelve hours and hadn't eaten all day. I had been
> asked questions at every opportunity, but I would
> always tell them that I wouldn't talk. Sometimes they
> would tell me about places in America where Japan
> had bombed and taken possession of property. Then
> they would come up very close to my face and open
> their mouths and laugh.
>
> I was then led into a room, and the blindfold was
> removed. A little Japanese [man] of stocky build was
> standing behind a table smoking a cigar, rubbing his
> hands together and talking really fast in Japanese.

Several others were in the room. The man behind the table said through the interpreter, "I am the kindest judge in all China. I want to treat you real good. Everywhere I have the reputation of being the kindest judge in all China."[65]

Jake stared at the fat fellow smoking the black cigar. The judge returned Jake's gaze and said, "You're very fortunate to be questioned by me. You just tell us what the truth is and I'll give you a nice glass of warm sweet milk." Jake was asked if Doolittle was his commanding office and answered, "I won't talk." Instead, Jake gave him his name, rank, and serial number, because that was all he was required to say under the Geneva Convention.[66] The judge responded to this by saying that Jake was Japanese property.[67]

The judge continued, "How do you pronounce h-o-r-n-e-t?" Jake responded, "That's *hornet.*" The judge replied, "That's the aircraft carrier you flew off of to bomb Japan?" Jake said, "I won't talk." The judge continued, "Sixteen B-25s took off the *Hornet* and bombed Japan. Is this true?" Jake continued to respond, "I won't talk." This must have angered the "kind" judge greatly because soon he struck the table with his fist, saying, "When you talk to me, you look me straight in the eye."[68]

The judge, growing angrier, pulled out his sword and held it up. Looking directly at Jake he said, "Tomorrow morning when the sun comes up, I'm going to cut your head off." Jake stood there silently. "What do you think of that?" the judge asked. Jake responded:

> I told him I thought it would be a great honor to me if the kindest judge in China cut my head off. The judge and others laughed for the first time, and a little later I was taken to my cell.
>
> I lay in the cell all night, blindfolded, handcuffed, without blankets. The next morning at sunrise I was led out of my cell. I had no breakfast. The blindfold was taken off, and the handcuffs were removed. I looked around for the judge with his weapon of execution. [Instead,] I saw a fellow with a camera, and everyone was smiling. After the picture was taken, I was loaded onto a Japanese two-motored transport. Again, I was

blindfolded, handcuffed, and tied with ropes. I could
hear some of my companions talking, but I was not
able to say anything to them.[69]

The pictures the Japanese took of the prisoners found their way into
Time magazine. When the magazine was published, Jake's mother and
brother, thousands of miles away, saw the photographs. His mother wondered if the man on the cover was indeed her son, Jake. Jake's younger
brother looked at the photo and said, "Yes, it's Jake, and he's mad."[70] Later,
Jake's mother would receive a letter from Colonel Doolittle, dated May
22, 1942. In the letter, Doolittle wrote, "I am extremely sorry to have to
bring you bad news. The latest information that we are able to get is that
your son landed near Japanese occupied territory and that two of the
crewmembers are missing and three have been taken prisoner. We are
unable to authenticate this report and also unable to determine which of
the crewmembers are missing and which captured. An attempt is being
made today through the Red Cross to obtain this information. I am sorry
that I am obliged to give you such an unfortunate report....I am proud
to have served with Jacob and I hope that I have the opportunity to serve
with him again."[71]

Soon, the men were flown from China to Tokyo for questioning. With
their leg cuffs on, they were taken in the cold to a room for questioning. Jake's legs began to shake. He tried to keep them from shaking, but
they did anyway. He did not like looking like he was scared. They asked
him many questions and Jake did not want to respond, only answering,
"I won't talk."

Over time, Jake realized they seemed to have a good deal of information about the Doolittle Raid. They even knew he was a bombardier. One
interrogator said, "You know all about the Norden bombsight....we want
you to draw us a picture of [it]...put the knobs on it and show us how
it's built." Jake responded that he could not draw. He drew some X's and
lines, but no bombsight. He told his inquisitors that they were unlucky for
capturing him because he could not draw anything, not even a picture of
a house.[72] However, in the meantime, one of the other men drew the Norden bombsight perfectly. When asked later if the picture was a Norden
bombsight, there was no use denying it, so Jake responded, "It sure is."[73]

Realizing they were getting nowhere with their four weeks of around-the-clock interrogation techniques, they decided to let the prisoners sleep at night. During the daylight, the questioning continued.

The Doolittle Raid had taken the Japanese by surprise. From the outset, General Hajime Sugiyama felt that the airmen were war criminals and should be dealt with severely. He argued that the "Air raids are a matter of strategic military operation. They should come under the jurisdiction of the military staff headquarters. All the investigations and punishments in regard to the raids will be conducted by our military staff headquarters in Tokyo."[74]

Finally, at the behest of General Shigera Sawada, commanding officer of the Japanese Thirteenth Army, an order was issued declaring that the eight men would stand trial in Tokyo. Fortunately, there were differences of opinion within military headquarters and the Japanese War Department. Sugiyama lobbied to sentence the American airmen to death. This, he believed, would send a stern message to the U.S. and possibly prevent further threats of this nature. However, then Premier of Japan, General Tojo, argued that Japan had no law imposing the death penalty on foreign soldiers who might be captured on Japanese soil. To this end, Tojo actually proposed such a law, which would impose the death penalty should Allied flyers be captured in Japan. Tojo believed this would deter future Allied air raids on Japan.[75]

While Japanese leaders were trying to decide how to proceed with the airmen, eighteen more days of interrogation continued. The Japanese wanted to find out where the Americans had gasoline storage sites in China. During this time, the men were unable to speak to each other, but found comfort in being able to hear each other's voices.

It was finally decided that the men should be tried in Shanghai. On the way, they stopped at Nagasaki. During the train journey, the prisoners were handcuffed, leg cuffed, and tied with rope. The journey was arduous and extremely uncomfortable. Their bodies ached as the rope dug into their skin. The handcuffs and leg cuffs were tightly clasped, preventing normal blood circulation, which made their arms and legs numb. While on the train, Jake remembered, "The coal soot from the train ride made us look as though we had been living in a pig sty."[76]

It had been almost two months since the men were captured. In that period, the Americans had been barely able to wash their faces with cold water. They had not bathed nor had a good night's sleep.

Arriving in Nagasaki, they were put in a prison cell with cold cement floors and a straw mat. The straw mat did little to shield the men from the chill emanating from the cement floors. Each room was damp and dark. Little natural sunlight entered the cell. The prison made one feel cut off from the outside world. In the corner of the room, there was a box. This small box acted as a toilet. The smell was revolting and the men could hardly stand to be next to it for more than a few seconds. The box was filthy as excrement oozed out of the sides. This unsanitary situation did little to prevent the spread of dysentery.

Despite the medieval conditions, the men took solace in the fact that they were all together. Jake and his crew almost forgot where they were as they learned the harrowing story of plane number six. The number six B-25 ran out of gasoline just as it reached the Chinese coastline. The pilot, Lieutenant Dean Hallmark, attempted to fly the plane over mountains, but the engines stalled. With the engines out and no fuel left, Hallmark guided the plane into the ocean. The landing itself was an incredible display of steel nerves and skill as he was able to put the large plane safely into the water. Once they had landed, they realized that their emergency life raft had been damaged. It was useless. The men, not wanting to spend an extra second on the plane for fear of it going under jumped into the ocean and began swimming for shore.[77]

Two of the crew, the bombardier and the rear gunner, were having trouble swimming. Lieutenant Dean Hallmark and Lieutenant Chase Nielsen were unaware that the others were having trouble so they continued on. Lieutenant Robert Meder heard the rear gunner struggling, so he turned around to help his crewmate. In an uncanny display of courage and stamina, Meder swam the entire night holding onto the rear gunner. Swimming through the night, his friend lost consciousness and his body went completely limp. Meder thought his friend had died, but he refused to let go. After hours of swimming, Meder reached the shore still holding the body of the rear gunner. He was exhausted and collapsed on the sand. A few hours passed and he awoke. On the beach he saw the bodies of the rear gunner and the bombardier. He went over to both men and attempted to revive them, but it was too late. The men had died either of hypothermia or wounds they received in the crash.[78]

The three survivors of number six were separated and had to make their way on their own. Each one did the best he could. When Lieutenant Nielsen reached the beach, he crawled to a bank to use as a shelter. As soon as he rolled over in the bank, he felt himself falling. Hitting the ground knocked him out and he lay unconscious for a while. When he regained his senses, he realized that he had fallen into a small canyon. He was lucky he had not broken his neck in the fall. Nielsen got up and noticed a trail, which he followed until he came to a small village.[79]

Lieutenant Hallmark remained on the beach until daylight as well. When daylight came, he began to wander around looking for his comrades. Not seeing anyone, he came across a trail and began to walk it. His entering the Chinese village caused a bit of commotion. To see an American soldier appear from the woods frightened the Chinese who quickly surrounded the weak American. The Chinese began asking him questions, but Hallmark had no idea what they were saying. They hurried the American into a small mud house and fixed him some hot tea. All of a sudden, one of the Chinese began speaking hurriedly and pointing at the door. Hallmark got the feeling that the man was warning him that someone was coming. Thinking that the man might be a Japanese soldier approaching, Hallmark quickly grabbed a large piece of wood and put it over his shoulder. As the door opened, Hallmark hoisted the wood and was ready to strike. To his surprise, in walked Lieutenant Nielsen! Hallmark dropped his weapon and greeted his crewmate.

In time, the Chinese also discovered Lieutenant Meder and all three were together again. The Chinese treated the Americans well, giving them food and allowing them to sleep. The airmen believed that their Chinese friends were going to help them escape from the Japanese. This turned out to be a misguided thought as the Chinese soldiers turned the Americans over to Japanese officials.[80]

After the miserable one-day experience in Nagasaki, Jake's crew was put on a train to Shanghai. There they joined the other captured Doolittle raiders and immediately were placed in the "Bridge House," one of Japan's infamous World War II prison camps. They arrived in poor physical condition. Their bodies were covered in scabs and sores. The scabs bled when they scratched them and the sores oozed a disgusting white liquid. They were emaciated and barely able to move. Also, they were not the only guests in this cell. They shared the room with fifteen Chinese prisoners, two of which were women.[81] The room was so small that they all could not lie down at the same time. This made the quarters cramped. Everybody reeked and the stench often made people gag and throw up. The floor of the room was infested with bedbugs, lice, and rats, which made sleeping nearly impossible.[82]

Food at the Bridge House was nothing to write home about. It consisted of a cup of boiled rice for breakfast, four ounces of bread at lunch, and four ounces of bread at dinner. It was now the summer of 1942 and temperatures were in the upper eighties. In the crowded cell, the airflow was limited and the heat was stifling. Water was also in short supply. Indeed, the eight Americans had to share two quarts of water a day, which is far less than the two and a half liters that is required for the body to maintain itself. Taking all of this in, Jake made a few observations about the jail and his captors:

> One day, one of the Chinese women fell down and hurt her head. They laughed and said she was pretending to be sick. Guards hit her on the head with a stick, which was attached to their keys. They seemed to be the very lowest type of people. Sometimes they would make us stand up during the night after they had awakened us from our sleep. They would threaten to hit us with long clubs, which they poked through the bars of the cell.
>
> It was the first time that I had ever been in such a wicked environment. I could not help wondering why there was so much difference between America and the Orient. There is bad in America, but the bad in America does not begin to compare with that which we observed. The truth was beginning to dawn upon me—it is Christianity that makes the difference. Even though many people in America do not profess to be Christians, yet they are following the Christian ways. Even the non-Christian people in America do not hit women over the head. The people who are Christians have shown the rest of the world the right way to act. It is because God has said Christians are to be the light of the world. I had always tried to steer away from religion, but now I was beginning to see that Christianity is a great benefit to mankind. It is God's plan for mankind's happiness.

In the daytime, we were supposed to sit straight up on the floor without any support for our backs. Often the guards would catch us leaning back on our elbows. There was always a quarrel as soon as we were caught. The guard would try to hit us on the head with a bamboo stick. The Chinese prisoners would allow themselves to be beaten and would then thank the Japanese guards. We always tried to talk the guards out of the notion of hitting us, but sometimes we would have to take the punishment.

One day, the guard caught Lieutenant Hite and Lieutenant Farrow leaning against the wall. He hollered, "Kurah!" (Hey!) and opened the door. His sword and steel scabbard were used to hit them on their heads. Lieutenant Hite grabbed the weapon, and the guard pulled his sword out of the scabbard. It looked as if Hite was going to be killed, but the guard finally calmed down and acted more human.

We weren't getting much food. Lieutenant Hallmark was a large man. His frame needed something to fill it up. We were all weak from the lack of water and food. One day, Lieutenant Hallmark passed out. He was very sick after that. We had to carry him to the toilet. He had dysentery, and we had to take him about every fifteen minutes. We had regular shifts, but it was too hard on us. Finally, all of us gave out. We were all lying flat on our backs from exhaustion and practically ready to give up.[83]

The eight Doolittle raiders lived in these conditions for seventy days. Along with the constant beatings, mistreatment, and the dirty and dank cell, the Americans knew absolutely nothing about their fate. Would they stay here forever, or would the Japanese government execute them? The men were dejected, discouraged, and losing all hope.[84]

It was during this time that the men went on trial, if that was what one could call it. The Americans stood before Major-General Shoji Ito, Chief Justice officer of the Japanese Thirteenth Army military court at

Shanghai. The trial was located in the tribunal courthouse and was led by chief prosecutor Major Itsura Hata. There were no defense attorneys, no declaration of innocence or guilt, and no witnesses. Indeed, the head-quarters at Tokyo had already decided the fate of the prisoners. General Sugiyama expected that the Americans would be sentenced to death and executed immediately.

The Americans stood accused of "indiscriminate bombing" during the Doolittle Raid over Japanese cities. The prosecution reported that the raids killed thousands of civilians and other non-military personnel. Hata also declared that the bombings violated military law.

At the end of the trial, the Americans were removed from the court-room. The judges returned the verdict. The Americans were to be executed. While the verdict was sent via telegram to Tokyo, the Americans did not know their fate.[85]

General Sugiyama was pleased with the death sentence. After all, he had argued from the beginning that the Americans should be dealt with harshly. The enemy could be shown no mercy, especially when they had bombed the Japanese homeland. However, there was a contingent in the imperial Japanese army who believed a death sentence was too severe at this stage in the war. Besides, there was a chance that the Japanese could gain valuable information from the Americans if they were kept alive.

In the meantime, the Americans languished in the Bridge House. The health of the eight continued to decline and reached the point where it was necessary to improve their living conditions or risk their deaths. After more than seventy days, the Japanese authorities decided that the Ameri-cans should be moved to another prison just outside of Shanghai.[86] The prisoners were given no reason as to why they were being moved. Once they reached their new quarters, the men continued to live in squalor just as before. This time there was an additional bonus, solitary confinement. Each man was placed in a cell about nine by five feet. No light entered the cell except when meals were delivered through an opening in the door. While in the cell, their imaginations raced. During the long nights in soli-tary confinement, the men grappled with the unknown. In their minds, they imagined the doors opening and being led outside to face a firing squad.

Unbeknownst to the men, there were rivalries and jealousies flaring up between Japanese army leaders and war cabinet officials. This impacted the final decision regarding their fate. Records show that Tojo was granted an audience with the emperor and informed him that he was in favor of a more lenient sentence, but that General Sugiyama had sentenced the men to death. In the end, the emperor commuted five of the mens' sentences to life in prison, while the remaining three—pilot Hallmark, pilot Farrow, and machine gunner Spatz—were to die by firing squad.

A message from General Sugiyama declared that the war criminals Hallmark, Farrow, and Spatz would die on October 15, 1942. Whether or not the executions were carried out on that day is unknown. What is known is that Hallmark, Farrow, and Spatz were led outside and blindfolded. They were then made to kneel on the ground. One by one they received a bullet to the head from a Japanese rifle. For some reason, the Japanese placed three crosses over their graves, which allowed the surviving Doolittle raiders to recover the bodies once the war was over.

The five spared were not aware that their comrades had been killed until after the war. The men sentenced to life in prison—Meder, Nielsen, Hite, Barr, and DeShazer—were hurried into a courtroom. The judge told them that they had been found guilty of war crimes and were to be executed. However, the emperor of Japan changed their sentence and they were to receive life imprisonment, instead. The judge also told them that they would receive "special treatment." What this entailed, the men did not know, but their imaginations ran wild. Following this statement, they were taken back to their rooms. After the verdict, Jake began to wonder, "I had expected to be executed from the way the Japanese had acted. It was really a relief to know that they were now planning to let us remain alive. I could not help feeling a strange sense of joy, even though solitary confinement and a long war awaited any possible chance of freedom. At the same time, it seemed almost hopeless to think of ever being free again, since the most probable thing would be that we would be executed when America did win the war."[87]

The doubt and fear each man faced was compounded when they returned to solitary confinement. It was here that the men would spend the next forty months.

Chapter 6

ALONE IN THE DARK

From my youth I have been afflicted and close to death;
I have suffered your terrors and am in despair.
—*Psalm 88:15*

SIX MONTHS HAD passed since the morning Jake and his comrades took off from the *Hornet*. How different were those days! Jake recalled the sense of adventure that the men experienced as they steamed toward Japan. He felt so important having been selected for such a mission. He remembered the day of their launch vividly—how the crew cheered when Colonel Doolittle got his B-25 in the air! He remembered the poor sailor who had his arm cut off by the propeller of his plane. Despite the anguish and pain he must have felt, he still had the gumption to tell Jake to give the enemy hell. And now Jake believed himself to be living in hell on earth.

Each man was placed in a cell measuring nine-by-five feet with no windows except a small opening near the ceiling. There were guards standing watch at the door. At times, they would come to taunt the prisoners. They were given no books, radios, or newspapers. They had no time for fellowship. They received no letters or packages from home.[88] They were alone, isolated. The men wondered if their families still believed them to be alive. Each day they lived in fear and apprehension that eventually they would be executed.

Life in solitary confinement was not much of an existence. The days felt as though they lasted forever. The men spent twenty-three and a half hours each day alone. The biggest excitement came in the half hour they had to exercise and wash themselves. The men were anxious to see how each of the others were doing. Although the guards kept a close watch on them, they would talk, trying to give one another a word of encouragement if they needed it.

All the time spent in solitary confinement had a way of sapping the life out of a person. Each man knew that the only way they would survive was if they kept thinking that they were going to be rescued. They had to have faith that the U.S. would defeat the Japanese and win the war. Although they tried to think these thoughts, the hours spent alone unnerved the men. One of Jake's crewmate, Bob Hite, described what the soldiers would do to pass the time:

> Our cells were horribly cold as the winter came on. The two blankets were not enough on the bare floor and we begged for more. We worried about the simplest of creature comforts, but most of those endless days and nights were spent thinking. We examined every little detail of our lives that we could recall. Most of the memories were pleasant, like the things we did as kids, our families, school days, friends, the little everyday things we all take for granted when we are living out in the world of people. Then we'd think about our personal shortcomings and wondered if we would ever again have the chance to do anything about them.
>
> Sometimes I wondered how long I could live with myself. There didn't seem to be much depth to me and I got pretty tired of myself and everything about me. I regretted not having done more with my life so that I would be a better companion to myself. Gradually, however, the cold became so intense we couldn't even think.[89]

To find out what happened to the other three men they attempted to strike up conversations with the guards. During this time, they befriended Caesar Luis dos Remedios, a half-Japanese, half-Portuguese interpreter for the Japanese guards who also happened to be a prisoner. The men tried to find out what had happened to their three comrades. Remedios knew little. What he did tell them was that their friends had been taken to another prison camp. The men anxiously asked Caesar if they, themselves, were to be executed. Caesar told the Americans that he had heard that they were to be executed, but the emperor had commuted their sentence. This relieved fears that the Japanese were merely lying to the men.[90]

Caesar would always try to find ways to talk with the men. The Japanese guards did not like this and if they found the men conversing they would walk up behind them and say, "Hanashi Yamai!" (Stop talking!) The guards would then hit them on the head with a wooden board or the scabbard of their sword.

On one occasion, Caesar told the airmen a particularly horrific tale. As Japan sought to conquer parts of China, the Japanese had taken a fair amount of Chinese prisoners. These prisoners were used to perform hard labor. The Japanese had a particular distaste for the Chinese since the former believed they were racially superior to the latter. So, the Japanese would have the Chinese prisoners dig huge ditches. This affair was done in the afternoon sun, when the heat was unbearable. After the ditches were ready, the Japanese made them kneel down with their hands bound behind their back. A blindfold was then placed over their eyes. A Japanese guard would stand over the prisoner, draw his *katana* and raise the sword over his head. Slowly and systematically, the Chinese prisoners were beheaded. The heads would roll into the ditch and then the bodies were thrown on top. Once they were executed, more Chinese prisoners were tasked with covering up the open graves.[91]

The men were horrified. Even if they did not want to believe it, they would sometimes see the Japanese guards with blood splattered all over their glasses. Indeed, the Japanese guards would walk up to the airmen with "blood on their glasses—'One day,' they said, they would cut off our heads and kick us in a ditch."[92]

Caesar would also find ways of sneaking extra food to them. One method he perfected was taking an extra spoonful of food out of his guard's dishes. When the guard was not looking, he would quickly add the food to the Americans' bowl. The risk Caesar was taking was great. If caught aiding the Americans, he likely would have been punished severely or even executed.[93]

Other ways the prisoners occupied the never-ending monotony was with games. Lieutenant Meder had come up with a game involving their meager food rations. The game went like this: each week they would draw a number, and the man with the winning number would receive an extra half of a bowl of rice or a bowl of soup.[94] Luck was on Jake's side as he made it a habit of winning the game. He noted, "We had lots of fun over this game, although it only lasted for two months and even then only once a week. We often used to agree in advance to trade a bowl of rice for two bowls of soup. When the food came, however, we would howl and complain about the other fellow being a sharp trader if we thought he got the best deal. We never knew, of course, in advance what the food was going to be, but it kept us amused to trade with one another."[95]

Another activity Jake occupied himself with was to climb his prison cell walls. Since the cell was only five feet wide, it was possible for him to gain a foothold in order to push himself up. While this required some trial and error, through proper maneuvering he could climb twelve feet to the ceiling. Jake's motivation for doing this was not just for physical exercise. Instead, he wanted to peer out of the small window at the top. When he reached the top, he could look out at the countryside. His eyes took in the scenery. While this undoubtedly helped boost Jake's spirits, it reminded him of the freedom that he was being denied by his Japanese captors. Fortunately for Jake, the guards never caught him scaling the walls of his prison cell.

In January of 1943, Lieutenant Hite became very ill. "He passed out cold, and when he came to several minutes later, he had double vision and couldn't move. An orderly was summoned and Hite was given a shot that knocked him out for forty-eight hours." By the time he woke up, Barr, Nielsen, and DeShazer were moved out of the cell, and Meder was left to take care of Hite.[96] "He remained sick for about three months. During this period, he became erratic, both in his conversation and in his actions. He did not return to normal until early spring."[97]

By April of 1943, the men were again relocated. They were flown to a prison in Nanking where the men were immediately returned to solitary confinement. However, they did find some relief in the move as the guards at Nanking seemed to be more receptive and friendlier. Sometimes the guards told the men about the war, something they were ordered not to do, but did anyway. The men would be taken outside for some exercise and to have the cells cleaned. Here, they managed to say hello and try to have brief conversations with one another. However, the guards did not permit this and would tell them to be quiet.

Time dragged on slowly. To keep their minds fresh, they created mental challenges from the planning of a future farm to the memorizing of a poem.[98] Sometimes they would have a wrestling match with their Japanese guards. When the guards won, they would shout, "Nippon banzai!

Nippon banzai!" (Japan wins! Japan wins!) Once in a while, they would
have a guard who would let them talk at length during their exercise period. When the Japanese spoke of the war to the men they insisted that the
Japanese were winning. The guards frequently told the men that there was
no hope for them. One guard said that Chicago had been bombed and
that Japanese forces had overtaken the White House. The men, although
dejected, refused to believe this propaganda.

What was made abundantly clear by the guards was that Japan was
ready to fight until the last man. The guards said that Japanese soldiers
possessed the *yamato damashii*, the "Japanese fighting spirit," which
would crush the weak Americans. They believed American society to be
weak and focused solely on pleasure and self-fulfillment. This, they said,
made it impossible for the Americans to resist Japanese imperial forces.
However, "If Japan should lose and America should win," the guards said,
"[the] prisoners would not be set free. Instead, they would all have their
heads cut off."[99] The guards also told the Americans that Japan's divine
emperor ensured their victory.

Through such conversations, the men learned about the Japanese
belief in the divine emperor. The Japanese believed that the emperor rep-
resented an unbroken kingly lineage that could be traced back to the sun
goddess Amaratsu. The emperor was revered as a "god-man," a being that
was fully man and fully divine. Because of the emperor's divinity, the
Japanese believed that he could not be wrong and that Japan's victory was
ensured. Moreover, since the emperor had asked the country to fight for
him in this military campaign, death in service of the emperor was the
greatest honor a Japanese soldier could achieve. Remembering these conversations, Jake said, "They would tell us many fantastic tales of how God
was on their side and how they were able to sink many ships with just one
airplane. It seemed to be their belief that they were in the right as far as
the war was concerned. They said that America had started the war. We
were greatly surprised when they brought out some of their arguments.
It seemed hard to understand how grown men could believe some of the
things the Japanese government was telling their people. However, these
men were convinced that they were in the right and that their country
was going to win. They had a confidence in a supernatural power that
was unshakeable. These 'Chinese-head-removers' said that they were in
the right and that God was always on the side of righteousness."[100]

The idea that the emperor was a god had an impact on Jake. Speaking of this belief, Jake added, "These men had never been taught about the true God. How could they know that the God who has been revealed for all mankind is on the side of peace? They did not know about Jesus, who died on the cross to pay the penalty for the sin of hatred and the lust for power. They did not know about the Spirit of Jesus who will enter into a person and take away the hatred and greed of this world. They had only been taught about a god who was seeking everything for Japan. They needed to know about Jesus who was God's true Representative for every nation and every generation of men."[101]

In late 1943, the men noticed that Lieutenant Meder had become increasingly weak and thin. He was suffering from the scourge of prison, dysentery. Worried about him, the men wanted to find out how he was, but no one dared approach him under the watchful eyes of the guards. Lieutenant Nielsen, however, decided that he had to check on his comrade. With blatant disregard for the rules, he walked over to Meder and asked him how he was feeling. Seeing this, a guard yelled at Nielsen to shut up, but Nielsen paid no attention to him. The guard continued to yell at Meder and Nielsen, who continued to talk to each other. When Nielsen finally appeared in front of the guard, the guard reared back and slapped him across the face. Nielsen slowly put his bucket on the ground and cleared his throat. In a deliberate movement, he reached out and smacked the guard with the back of his hand.

It as an unbelievable sight as the guard stood there and turned red with anger. What would happen next was anyone's guess. Seven or eight guards ran over to the scene. They all sucked air through their teeth to show their displeasure. Meanwhile, the guard reached for his steel scabbard and started to swing at Nielsen. However, the guard's strokes were sloppy and Nielsen was able to dodge them.[102] As Jake noted, "It was comical to see the way Nielsen dodged the blows of the angry guard. One swing would have killed him if the guard had made contact. One of the guards who had been watching tried to stop the fight and was rewarded for his good intentions with a strike to the back of his head with the scabbard. After that, the fight ended."[103]

After the ruckus, the men were taken to their cells. Jake wondered what would happen to Nielsen. To openly defy a guard like that could carry a death sentence. To their surprise, nothing happened to Nielsen. Indeed, the entire incident was forgotten. It appeared that the guards actually admired Nielsen for his courage.

Weeks passed and the condition of Lieutenant Meder worsened. Sadly, Lieutenant Meder died on December 1, 1943, from complications of beriberi. The men were not informed of Meder's death immediately, but became aware of it when a large box was being constructed in the yard. In speaking of Meder, Jake said, "Lieutenant Meder seemed to understand the Bible message well. He and I had a good talk one day while we were pulling weeds out in the yard. Meder told me that Jesus Christ is the Lord and coming King, that Jesus is God's Son and that God expects the nations and people to recognize Jesus as Lord and Savior. He said that the war would last until Jesus Christ caused it to stop. I did not understand what he meant at the time, but I remembered his words later. Lieutenant Meder had a brilliant mind. He was truly a gentleman in every way, and he was a prince of a fellow."[104]

The next day, the men were taken to Meder's cell for a last look. There was a box with a nice wreath of flowers and a Bible on the lid of the box. Once news of Meder's death reached the higher-ups, changes were initiated on how to treat the prisoners. They were given bread along with their daily rations of rice and soup and meals increased from two to three a day. Soon, the health and spirits of the four prisoners improved.

The prisoners also requested something to stimulate their minds. The Japanese complied and gave them a few books, one being an American Standard Edition of the Bible. Since Jake was the only non-officer in the group, he had to wait his turn for the books. It was not until the beginning of summer 1944 that he had the chance to read the Bible. From the moment he got his hands on the Bible, his life was never the same.

Chapter 7

FILLED WITH JOY

For he has rescued us from the dominion of darkness
and brought us into the kingdom of the Son he loves, in
whom we have redemption, the forgiveness of sins.
—*Colossians 1:13*

IT WAS MAY 1944 when Jake finally received the Bible. He had waited patiently for his turn and now it finally came. The guard came to his cell and gave him an American Standard Edition of the Bible. Here it was. In those three weeks, Jake voraciously read the Bible. Jake recalled that he felt like a young boy who had opened a birthday or Christmas present.

Having grown up in a Christian home, Jake was familiar with the Bible. His parents, good Christian people, had quoted Scripture to him and he also heard it when he was young and in Sunday school at the Free Methodist Church. However, up to that point in his life, the Bible was only a book. It had no real significance to him. He had heard his parents and pastor describe the book over and over again as the Word of God, but until then he did not realize what that meant.

Jake took the book from the guard. As he sat in his cell and read, he did not have much light and the print was terribly small, but this did not matter much because now he had something to read. He opened the Bible at Genesis 1:1 and read, "In the beginning God created the heavens and the earth. Now the earth was formless and empty, darkness was over the surface of the deep, and the Spirit of God was hovering over the waters. And God said, 'Let there be light,' and there was light."[105] He was amazed at what he read. Jake learned about God's Creation of the universe and how He made the earth out of an empty void. How He brought the day and night, and creatures to dwell on the land and in the sea. He read about how God created Adam and Eve, and how they lived for a time with

God in paradise. He learned about pride, the sin that fed man's desire to be like God, causing the eventual expulsion of humans out of the Garden of Eden.

He began to encounter the great biblical figures Abraham, Sarah, Moses, Isaiah, and Jeremiah. Jake read the story of God's deliverance of the Israelites out of the hands of their Egyptian captors with relish. He was particularly impressed with how God appeared to Moses as a burning bush. Here was a God who made Himself manifest to human beings. God spoke to the prophets and kings of Israel and when God spoke, they listened. He also found it fascinating how the Israelite prophets foretold Jesus' coming. He remembered reading Isaiah 53:5–6, which states, "But he was pierced for our transgressions, he was crushed for our iniquities; the punishment that brought us peace was upon him, and by his wounds we are healed. We all, like sheep, have gone astray, each of us has turned to his own way; and the LORD has laid on him the iniquity of us all."

In those three weeks, Jake voraciously read the Bible. He committed as much as he could to memory so that, in hard moments, he could find comfort in the sacred Word of God. Reflecting on the Bible, Jake had this to say:

> The Bible is different from any other book that has been written. The men who wrote the Bible said that God spoke to them and [history] has proved that God did speak to them. These men wrote down what God revealed to them. The prophets foretold the greatest event that ever happened in the history of mankind. They foretold the coming of God's Son, Jesus Christ, the Savior for all the people of the world.
>
> Other books do not make the claim that God spoke to their authors. They couldn't prove that God spoke to them if they did not make such a claim. The Bible has proof that God did speak to the Bible writers. The events they proclaimed came to pass—even the event of deity coming to our world was known to these men. Since God spoke to them, we know that the Bible is true. It contains God's plan for our salvation. The supernatural power that created this world has given a revelation to all mankind so that we can

know truth. God has revealed His power through the manifestation of the universe. He has spoken to mankind and given them His law. The Bible is not man's reasoning. It is God's Word.

The Jewish people made sacrifices of cattle, sheep, goats, and fowl for the purpose of making atonement for their sins. The prophets told the people that we have all sinned. Every person does something wrong. God made us to be perfect, but, because man had fallen from the perfect state in which God made him, we are all imperfect. Imperfection is no glory to God. Our imperfection is displeasing to God.

However, God is willing to forgive us if we have faith in Him. To show that they had faith in God, the Jewish people made sacrifices for atonement of their sins. Of course, the prophets knew that these sacrifices of animals would never satisfy the law of God, which says that the person must die if he sins. However, the prophets knew that the death of God's Son would make an atonement for all sins ever committed in this world if people showed that they had faith to believe in God. The sacrifice of animals was the means God had given to the Jewish people of the Old Testament age for a sign of faith. Some of the Jewish prophets saw the salvation plan of God clearly. To some of the people, God revealed just enough for them at that particular time.[106]

For Jake, the evidence that this was God's Word was overwhelming. Indeed, he realized how the prophecies in the Old Testament came about in the New Testament. For instance, he was astounded at how accurately the prophet Isaiah predicted the suffering of the coming Messiah. With the words of Isaiah in the back of his mind, Jake read the story of Jesus' crucifixion in Matthew 27. Isaiah said that the people would revile and reject the Messiah. This, Jake thought, was because the Jewish people believed that the Messiah was to be a warrior king who would come and forcibly deliver them from the Romans much the same way as Moses rescued the Israelites from the Egyptians. However, Jesus did not meet these expectations. Instead of a warrior, He was a Healer and Teacher. He spoke in the temples, drove out demons, performed miracles, and associated with tax collectors, harlots, and lepers.

Jake began to understand why the Jewish people believed Jesus to be a fraud. From their vantage point, God had forsaken Jesus and had allowed Him to die a horrible and gruesome death. However, as Jake read the Gospel, he believed that Jesus was the fulfillment of that which the Old Testament prophets predicted. He recalled the words of Daniel, "The Messiah shall be cut off" (Dan. 9:26, NKJV) and Zechariah, "Smite the shepherd, and the sheep shall be scattered" (Zech. 13:7, KJV).

He found continuity between the Old and New Testaments. He thought about this at length, "Yes, Christ died for us. That is the message all the way through the Bible. Many different people were writing, but the same revelation of salvation was given to every one. The same thread of thought is carried from Genesis to Revelation. I've seen proof of it in my lifetime. I've seen the handiwork of God. God has manifested Himself for us to see."[107]

Jake spent as many hours as he could reading and digesting God's Word. Later, as a student at Seattle Pacific College (S.P.C.), he described to his early biographer and then-president of S.P.C., Dr. Hoyt Watson, how he would go back and forth between the Old and New Testaments, each time gleaning some new insight. He began to see all too clearly that the Old Testament paved the way for the coming of Jesus in the New Testament. The hours spent reading and meditating on the Bible were having an effect on him in that Japanese prison cell. As Jake noted:

> God made it very plain that a Savior was needed and that a Savior was coming. As the prophets foretold, the Savior was born in Bethlehem. Jesus, the Savior, lived in Bethlehem. Jesus, the Savior, lived a sinless life. He performed many great miracles.
>
> Jesus made it clear that He is the "Christ, the Son of the living God" (Matt. 16:16). He was the One the prophets had made so many statements about. Jesus told the people that He existed before Abraham, who had lived nearly two thousand years previously. In John 17:5, Jesus tells of the glory, which He had with

the Father before the world was created. Jesus boldly claimed to be God, to which the Jewish people reacted by picking up stones to stone Him. When Jesus asked them the reason for their desire to stone Him, they said it was blasphemy as He made out that He himself was God (John 10:33).

Some of the Jewish leaders became angry at Jesus' teachings. He was different from any other person that had been in the world before. He is the only one who could fill the position of the Messiah. There never will be anyone else that can truthfully make the statements that Jesus made; for instance, "I am the resurrection, and the life: he that believeth in me, though he were dead, yet shall he live" (John 11:25, KJV). It must have been astounding blasphemy to many of the Jews to see a man stand up and make such a claim.

A few of the Jewish leaders gathered a mob, which caught Jesus and received permission to crucify Him. Jesus was nailed to the cross as it was foretold in prophecy. They drove nails through His hands and feet. David had written about this in Psalm 22. It was a shameful death that the wicked mob forced upon Jesus. Two thieves were crucified with Him. The Roman soldiers and the people made fun of Jesus and tortured Him, but God allowed all this to happen to His Son that people might be saved.

They took Jesus down from the cross, and three days later Jesus arose from the grave and appeared to His followers. They had searched for Him in the grave, but they could not find Him. One day, a short time after His Resurrection, His disciples were in a room where the windows were shut and the doors were all locked. Jesus came into that room. He was super-natural. The walls could not stop Him. Jesus showed His followers the holes in His hands, which the nails had caused when He hung from the cross. He showed

them the hole in His side when they pierced Him
with the spear while He was on the cross. Jesus was
showing Himself to His followers to prove that He is
"the resurrection and the life" (John 11:25, KJV). He
showed Himself to more than five hundred people at
one time. On one occasion, Jesus was talking to His
disciples and, while He was talking, He was parted
from them and taken into the sky. He disappeared in
the clouds.[108]

While in that cell reading the Bible, Jake began to remember his days
as a youth when he attended that small and vibrant Methodist church. He
began to recall what he learned in Sunday school or a particular sermon
preached by the minister. Although we are not privy to his thoughts while
he was in solitary confinement, what we do know is that God's Holy Spirit
was visiting and comforting Jake during his time of need. Jake began to
be convinced that the Bible was God's Word and that Jesus' Resurrection
was a turning point in human history. He noted:

This is the greatest event that has happened in the
history of mankind. It is of more importance to us
than anything else. It is the only time that God has
raised a man from the grave. Why was God so particular to raise Jesus from the grave? Why did God single
Him out of all the millions of people? Obviously, the
reason is that Christ was the Son of God.

God put His seal on Jesus Christ through the sign
of prophecy and through the sign of the resurrection
from the dead. Both of these facts agree. God has
scientifically proved to all mankind that Jesus Christ
is our Savior. Anyone who can read can search out
the Messiah. He boldly stands out from all others!
The Bible is a wonderful book!

There is no reason for me to doubt the fact of the
Resurrection of Jesus. The men relating these events
gave us truthful accounts. They were men who would
not tell a lie. They believed that liars would receive

punishment in hell's fire throughout eternity. Their soul's salvation depended on their telling the truth. The Bible tells us that liars will be cast into hell. They would have been awful hypocrites to profess faith in Jesus and then tell the public a big lie.

When we read their writings and see how they gave their lives in martyrdom, we know that they were not liars. Men of such caliber do not lie. Jesus Christ, who knew all things, had made the statement that His "Words will never pass away" (Matt. 24:35). We can be assured that we have a truthful account of the gospel in the Bible.[109]

On June 8, 1944, as Jake would recount years later to Dr. Watson, he sat on a stool with the Bible opened on the cold ground of the cell and began to read Romans. Hunching over the stool, he stopped at Romans 10:9. He read it, "That if you confess with your mouth, 'Jesus is Lord,' and believe in your heart that God raised him from the dead, you will be saved." He had read this passage many times before, but now it took on a new importance and meaning. Immediately, he felt compelled to pray. In prayer Jake said, "Lord, You know all things. You know I do repent of my sins. Even though I am far from home and though I am in prison, I must have forgiveness."[110] He would later tell church audiences that this was the exact moment when he accepted Christ. Reflecting on that moment many years later, he said that he had made human beings the boss of his life. As a Doolittle raider, Colonel Doolittle was Jake's boss. As a Christian, he now recognized that Jesus had become the 'Boss of his life.' In recalling his conversion experience on that day, he said:

> My heart was filled with joy. I wouldn't have traded places with anyone at that time. Oh, what a great joy it was to know that I was saved, that God has forgiven me of my sins and that I had become "partaker of the divine nature" (2 Pet. 1:4, KJV). Though I was unworthy and sinful, I had "redemption through his blood, the forgiveness of sins, in accordance with the riches of God's grace" (Eph. 1:7).

Hunger, starvation, and a freezing cold prison cell
no longer had horrors for me. They would be only
for a passing moment. Even death could hold no
threat when I knew that God had saved me. Death
is just one more trial that I must go through before
I can enjoy the pleasures of eternal life. There will
be no pain, no suffering, no sorrow, no loneliness in
heaven. Everything will be perfect with joy forever. I
had the promise of being like Jesus who is God's Son.
In that day, I will know all things, for I will then be a
partaker of immortality.[111]

Accepting Christ as his Savior and becoming a Christian did not
change Jake's immediate circumstances. He was still a prisoner of war
and lived in terrible conditions. The only difference now was that he made
up his mind that he was going to do his best to live life the way Christ
commanded him to live. He remembered how full of hate he was toward
his captors.

Just one day before his conversion, he became upset with a Japanese
guard. Jake had orders to clean his cell and the guard stopped by to see
Jake's progress. Jake, weakened by malnutrition, was taking a short rest
from his chore to regain his strength. The guard did not like this and
began yelling, "Hurry up!" at Jake. This made Jake angry and he jumped
to his feet and told the guard in English to "Go jump in the lake!"[112] The
guard, feeling insulted, immediately confronted the prisoner. As Jake recalled, "Before I knew what was going to happen, the door was unlocked,
and the guard hit me on the head with his fist. I immediately kicked him
in the stomach with my bare foot, and he hit me with his steel scabbard.
I had been using some water on the floor to mop up my cell. I picked up
the dirty mop water and threw it on the guard. It cooled him off enough
so that he didn't do any more than swear at me. But it is strange that he
didn't cut off my head. This was not the way that I had been taught to
make friends."[113]

Jake emphasized that this incident took place before Jake became a
Christian. After his conversion, Jake believed that he had to replace hate
for his captors with love. He wanted to follow Jesus' example by loving his
enemy. As fate would have it, he would have another opportunity to test
his newfound faith a few days later.

One day, an opportunity to demonstrate his faith appeared. Jake was being taken back to his cell by one of the guards after a short exercise period, and the guard started pushing him. "Hayaku! Hayaku!" (Hurry up! Hurry up!) the guard shouted as he slapped him on the back with his hand. When he came to the door of Jake's cell, he held it open a little and gave him a final push through the doorway. Before he could get all the way in, he slammed the door and caught his foot. He held the door against his bare foot and kicked it with his hobnailed shoes. Jake pushed against the door to get his foot free, and then jumped aside. The pain in his foot was severe, and he thought some bones were broken.

As he sat on the stool in great pain, he felt as if God were testing him somehow. He felt anger and resentment toward the guard and thought, "Surely God doesn't expect us to love the real mean ones in this world." But then he remembered the words of Jesus in Matthew 5:44 who said, "Love your enemies, bless those who curse you, do good to those who hate you, and pray for those who spitefully use you and persecute you" (NKJV).[114] Jake also remembered 1 Corinthians 13:4–8, the great love chapter, stating, "Love is patient, love is kind. It does not envy, it does not boast, it is not proud. It is not rude, it is not self-seeking, it is not easily angered, it keeps no record of wrongs. Love does not delight in evil but rejoices with truth. It always protects, always trusts, always hopes, always perseveres. Love never fails."

The incident helped Jake to understand what it really means when Christians are called to love their enemy. At that moment, Jake decided to replace all the hatred in his heart with love. He also wanted to try this new approach on the guard. When that same guard came to Jake's cell the following day, Jake bid him *"Ohayoo gozaimasu"* (Good morning). Jake chose not to curse or to hate, but rather to love. The guard looked confused and must have thought Jake had spent too much time in solitary confinement, but after many days of trying to be nice to the guard, the guard finally smiled and began to talk with Jake—as much as they could with Jakes' poor Japanese language skills.[115] The guard changed his attitude toward Jake and from that moment on he no longer shouted or treated Jake rudely. On one occasion, the guard slid a boiled sweet potato into Jake's cell. This was a wonderful treat. Trying to comprehend the great transformation that took place within him and what was happening in his cell, Jake told Dr. Watson:

How easy it was to make a friend out of an enemy because I had just tried. God's way will work if we try it out. Jesus was not an idealist whose ideals could not be realized. When He told us to love one another, He told us the best way to act, and it will work. His way will work out better than any other way which could be tried, but people and nations still try some other way to their own confusion.

It was easy to tell that my nature had changed. I had a different attitude toward life. It had all come about through the promises in the Bible. When we see those promises and know that they are true, our nature will be changed if we submit to God's will and accept Jesus. I had met the conditions in the promises, and I knew that God would do His part. God has promised to come and dwell in our hearts. First John 4:15 says, "Whosoever shall confess that Jesus is the Son of God, God dwelleth in him, and he in God" (KJV). I had confessed that Jesus is the Son of God, and God was dwelling in my heart.

There was a new power in my life. I had been weak in self-control and willpower, but now I had power so that I could even love my enemies. It all came from heaven. I knew that it was supernatural. Jesus had gone to heaven, and He is existing in the form of God in heaven now. His Spirit comes right into our hearts when we are obedient to Him and confess that He is the Son of God. We make friends with God and God loves us and delights in us. The Bible says in John 1:12, "As many as received him, to them gave he power to become the sons of God, even to them that believe on his name" (KJV). It is God that gives the power after we meet certain specified conditions. With the Spirit of Jesus dwelling in our hearts, we are able to love our fellow men. The world needs Jesus. We need to recognize God's Son. Without Jesus Christ we have hatred and terrible wars.

We all know that wars lead to hardship and heart-ache. We hate war, but we still continue to fight. As individuals, we often have the same trouble, for we know what is the right thing to do, but we lack the willpower or the self-control to go ahead and do what we know is right. I observed this when I was on the airplane leaving Japan at the time of the bombing. Long before that time, I had made up my mind not to shoot at civilians, but in spite of my resolutions I had shot at civilians. It is wrong to do things that are harmful to the body. It is wrong to be resentful and provoke others. I had often wished that I could live a life which was free from doing those things that I knew were wrong. But sin had brought constant defeat in my life throughout the years.

It was a great joy to me to find Jesus and to learn that He gives power to overcome such a defeated life. Herein lies the difference between a Christian and a person who is not a Christian. A Christian is "cleansed from all unrighteousness" (1 John 1:9). A Christian lives a victorious life. The power Jesus provides keeps us from doing what we know is wrong. Jesus gives self-control and willpower to all people who are weak on these points. By living such a victorious life, we have the witness that we know Jesus.[116]

Chapter 8

PERSEVERANCE IN PRISON

*Not only so, but we also rejoice in our sufferings, be-
cause we know that suffering produces perseverance.*
—Romans 5:3

WHILE HE HAD found spiritual fulfillment in solitary confinement, it had been twenty-six months since the Japanese
captured Jake and his crewmates. The captured Doolittle
raiders were now in poor physical condition. The summer heat of Nanking did little to raise their spirits. Indeed, the summer of 1944 was
terribly hot. The cramped wooden prison cells became unbearable. The
doors of the prison cells were made of solid wood without an opening to
allow outside air to circulate. From noon to about three in the afternoon,
the cell became stifling and the men found it hard to breathe.

It was during this Nanking heat wave when Lieutenant Hite took ill
with a high fever. The Japanese guards were concerned about him because
they did not want to be reprimanded like they were for Lieutenant Meder's death. They put a screen door in place of his wooden door to help
circulate the air better, but he remained ill. Even the Japanese officials
were concerned and ordered a physician to monitor Hite and bring him
back to health. Jake recalls that he could often hear the Japanese brining
cold towels and ice to put on Hite's feverish head.[117] The physician actually moved into the prison himself so that he could more closely monitor
Hite's condition.[118] Under the watchful eye of the young physician and the
cooling of temperatures as summer ended, Hite began to heal.

The long days and unbearable nights during that summer in 1944 left
Jake with much to think about. As he later told Dr. Watson, he had come
a long way in the span of a few months, from feelings of fear and dejec-
tion to the newfound joy of one who had accepted God's forgiving love. It
had been months since Jake had read the Bible, however his mind would

often recall his favorite passages. Of particular importance to Jake was the first Epistle of John. Indeed, he had memorized all five chapters and often meditated on them. Jake liked the first Epistle of John because it spoke plainly about sin and forgiveness. As 1 John 2:1–3 says, "My dear children, I write this to you so that you will not sin. But if anybody does sin, we have one who speaks to the Father in our defense—Jesus Christ, the Righteous One. He is the atoning sacrifice for our sins, and not only for ours but also for the sins of the whole world."

Through Jake's conversion, he had accepted Christ's atoning sacrifice for his sins. He felt like a new person. Jake also understood that God required obedience. As 1 John 2:5–6 reminded him, "But if anyone obeys his word, God's love is truly made complete in him. This is how we know we are in him: Whoever claims to live in him must walk as Jesus did." Jake found this passage instructive and thought, "That's a good method to tell whether anyone is a Christian. Anyone who keeps God's commandments is a Christian. I have faith that the blood of Jesus covers all of my sins. I know that Jesus died for me, consequently I can ask myself the question, 'Am I doing what I think is right to the best of my ability or am I doing anything that I know is wrong, willfully?' If I am not willfully disobedient and I am trying to do what I know to be right, I am living up to all the light that God has given me. I am keeping His commandments and the Bible says that I know Him if I keep His commandments."[119]

With autumn came more moderate temperatures. While the summer heat enervated the men, the brisk fall wind seemed to lift their spirits a bit. Their cells cooled substantially and made the time spent alone more bearable. In a few weeks, winter arrived with gusto. There came a heavy snow fall in December. As it turned out, this would be the coldest winter that the men spent in prison. The tattered rags the men had worn in the summer were not sufficient to keep them warm. The guards brought the men heavier clothes and even gave them back their uniforms to wear.[120]

The men dressed in as many layers as possible. One major improvement in this prison was the absence of lice. In the other prison, lice infested their cells and clothing. The lice were constantly crawling on their skin, which made it very difficult to sleep. Although the men developed a game hunting the lice by catching them in their clothes and then crushing them between their fingernails, they did not miss the pesky insects.

On one occasion, the men were taken outside to exercise while their cells were being cleaned. They were told not to take their shoes (Japanese slippers) off when they were exercising. This became difficult for them to do as they fell off easily and they needed to move fast to get warmed up. So they ignored the order and kicked off the shoes and started running barefoot in the frozen mud and snow. Once the guards noticed their bare feet, they ordered the men inside. The men thought they would be able to clean their feet at the water hydrant, but the guards told them to wash them outside in the snow.

Lieutenant Barr thought this was unacceptable. There was no way to wash your feet in the snow, all that would do was to numb their feet. Barr tried to walk past the guard in defiance. The guard grabbed his coat sleeve and tried to turn him around. Barr, a big man at six-feet-two inches tall, would have none of this. As the guard was pushing Barr, he cocked his elbow and delivered a blow to the guard's stomach.

The humiliated guard stumbled back and began to scream at Barr. Jake and the rest of the crew were rushed inside while Barr was kept outside to face about ten guards. The guards began to beat him. Barr was a physically tough man and did his best to dodge the guards and throw in a few more elbows and kicks. The guards had a rough time subduing Barr, but they were finally able to shove him inside and put him in his cell. To punish Barr's insolence, the guards placed him in a straight jacket with his arms tied behind his back and ropes around him so tight that his shoulders almost broke.[121] The ropes also constricted Barr's chest and created a terrible tension that made it hard to breathe. He screamed so loud the other men thought he was being killed.

Barr's screaming had a powerful impact upon the prisoners as well as some of the Japanese guards. One of the guards, Mr. Misaka, whom Jake described as a kindhearted and tender-spirited man, persuaded his colleagues to release Barr.[122] After an hour of this torture, the other guards complied. The guards told Barr that he should feel lucky because they tortured their own men by that means from four to six hours when they had to be disciplined.[123]

The whole incident left the men feeling dejected and hopeless. The men wondered how much more abuse they could take. Their thoughts inevitably turned to the war. How was the U.S. faring? The guards kept saying that the Japanese army and navy were embarrassing the Americans. While their stories always sounded exaggerated to the captured Americans, they were beginning to have doubts. These doubts were erased on December 25, 1944. Jake and the crew saw and heard U.S. bombers. While this was most unwelcome news to their captors, the crew was thrilled. It meant that American bombers had reached Nanking. What a turn of events! As the bombers approached, the Japanese could be heard shooting back. Soon, the men heard bombs exploding and saw great clouds of smoke in the distance.

Their satisfaction grew when they realized that they were deep in Chinese territory. For months upon months, the guards had gloated about how the U.S. had suffered defeat after defeat, including stories such as the Japanese having taken possession of San Francisco, New York, and had destroyed Washington D.C. The Japanese appeared surprised to see the bombers. They believed every bit of propaganda released by the Japanese government. The guards tried to adjust to the situation by telling the Americans that the U.S. had dropped a few bombs in the river, killing a handful of fish.[124]

Even the satisfaction of knowing that the bombers were close did not change the fact that the winter was extremely cold and that the men were sick and suffering with colds. On top of that, Jake broke out in huge boils. He counted seventy-five all over his body. At one point he became delirious and a Japanese medical officer was called. The officer gave him vitamin shots and they came with good food to help nourish him back to health.[125]

In the middle of June 1945, the men began one last journey. They were taken out of their cells, handcuffed and hooded, and put on a northbound train. On the train, each man had a guard. Their hands and legs were tied with belts and each man wore a green raincoat. Over their heads was a hat that had an attached mask, which covered the men's faces. The train was crowded. Most of the passengers were soldiers, but there were also some civilians. The women sat on the floor in the aisles or atop their baggage. Japanese men were the sole occupants of the seats.

The passengers were surprised to see prisoners wearing masks, but no one asked any questions. Jake remembers one incident with amusement, "A Japanese mother brought her two children up rather close to our masked faces. While the children were looking at us with surprised faces, the mother for sheer fun silently moved away. As the children looked at us and our peculiar masks, they screamed out in fright. This caused everyone in the train to laugh, and the mother returned smiling to comfort her children."[126]

Even in this situation, Jake realized that he was ever mindful of God's presence, "While riding on the train, I remembered the Bible message. I wondered what God was going to do with all these souls as these people didn't know Jesus. They probably never heard of Him. I thanked God for His mercy to me in allowing me the privilege of reading the Bible. I was glad for a Christian home and my parents' prayers, which God had heard. I wished there was some way the people on the train could know about the salvation, which God had provided for all people. What joy they would know if Jesus were dwelling in their hearts as he was dwelling in mine!"[127]

After three long days of traveling, the guards told them that they had arrived in Peking. After getting off the train, the men were taken to a shady place to wait because it was hot. As the Japanese soldiers milled about, it was evident that they held contempt for their Chinese counterparts. In one such example of this hatred, an old Chinese woman struggled to manage the many bags that she was carrying. A group of Japanese soldiers were approaching her. The Japanese expected the Chinese woman to immediately get out of the way. However, the bags she carried were heavy and her frail body was unable to move quickly enough. She could not get out of the way. The soldiers yelled and approached the woman. Instead of trying to help her with her luggage, the Japanese soldier grabbed her and slapped her twice across the face. This would motivate the woman to collect her bags and get out of the way. Seeing this treatment, Jake thought, "It made me wish that they [the Japanese] could be shown the way of love."[128]

They were then taken by truck to a military prison in Peking that housed more than one thousand Japanese prisoners. The conditions were not great. The Americans noticed that five or six Japanese prisoners were placed in a prison cell together and for two hours were forced to kneel on the floor without changing position.[129] After this they were made to stand up straight without resting their backs against the wall.

The Japanese guards bragged about how Japan was the leading nation in the world for decency and standard of living. After seeing China, Jake could see why the Japanese felt they lived better than the Chinese. However, in an effort to depict some balance, the Americans tried to tell the guards what life was like in U.S., "We tried to tell them about the food and the automobiles, but it seemed like a fairy tale to them. They thought America was a place where bandits flourished and waxed rich. Soldiers in the Japanese army are accustomed to being slapped by an officer of higher rank. When we told them there was no slapping in the U.S.

Army, they said that was impossible, for they thought there would be no discipline."[130]

This prison had one major drawback in that there was no courtyard. During their time in Nanking, the men had grown to love the courtyard. It allowed them to see and interact with one another and it gave them something to look forward to. Now, however, the Americans were isolated from each other. Each was placed in a solitary cell. The guards let them know that they would no longer be going outside for exercise. The only time they saw each other was when they got together for a bath once a week.

Chapter 9

A BITTER TASTE OF DEATH

Even though I walk through the valley of the shad-
ow of death, I will fear no evil, for you are with
me; your rod and your staff, they comfort me.

—*Psalm 23:4*

IN PEKING, THE prisoners were immediately placed in solitary confinement. At first they were forced to sit on the floor, just like the
other prisoners. The floor was hard and because they were emaciated
their bones would get extremely sore after short periods on the ground.
The pain became so unbearable that the guards decided to provide some
relief.

Jake remembered the relief the guards gave them. It took the form
of a small wooden stool, which had a top made of a two-by-four, about
eight inches long.[131] Throughout the day, the men were made to sit on this
uncomfortable piece of furniture. Although it was better than the floor,
it still pained the men nonetheless. According to their captors, the men
had to keep the stool three feet from the wall as they faced the rear wall.
Indeed, the Japanese did not want the Americans to witness the harsh
treatment their own soldiers received.[132]

Already in a weakened condition, Jake's health became worse just one
month after he arrived. He became sick with dysentery and boils appeared
all over his body.[133] Being unable to sit on his stool, he stayed on his bed
mat day after day. After three weeks of this suffering, he became delirious. He noted his condition in this way, "I still kept going over the verses
in the Bible that I had memorized. I thought it wouldn't be long before I
would be in heaven with Lieutenant Meder. My heart was hurting and I
could remember how Lieutenant Meder said his heart had hurt before he
died. Several of the Nanking guards had told me that the reason Meder

died was that his heart had stopped. I thought I would probably die for the same reason."[134]

Jake had these experiences for several days. One day, Matthew 17:20 came to his mind and he thought about it, "If you have faith as small as a mustard seed, you can say to this mountain, 'Move from here to there' and it will move. Nothing will be impossible for you." He began to think how small a mustard seed was and said to himself, "Surely I have that much faith that God can make me well!"[135]

From that day on, Jake said that he felt that the Holy Spirit was visiting him. He described a voice that penetrated his thoughts as he later noted, "I had often wondered where a person's thoughts come from and as I sat in prison I used to be conscious of the activity of my thoughts. Ordinarily, I had control over them, but now it was different. I still had control over my thoughts, yet I knew that I was being possessed by another power. I was sure I was not responsible for the thoughts coming to my mind. I had never dreamed of anything like this. It was hard for me to realize that I was experiencing such a glorious contact with God. 'It is the Holy Spirit who is speaking to you,' the mysterious voice said, 'the Holy Spirit has made you free.' I immediately began to wonder if I was going to get out of prison. The voice said, 'You are free to do as you please. You can go through the wall or jump over the wall, you are free.' I couldn't figure that out, but I never made any attempt to jump over the wall. I knew that I was free, but I had only a desire to do what was pleasing to God. 'The Holy Spirit has set you free from sin,' I was told."[136]

Jake began to ask God to heal his broken body. He also had the experience of having questions that would then be answered. For instance, he began to wonder whether he should continue to eat the food the guards were giving him. He would pray to God and receive guidance right away. As Jake said, "This was a big help to me in connection with my food. I was always hungry, but, often, if I ate the food, I would become very sick. When the food came to the door, I would pray and ask if I should eat the food or should I send it back. If the voice said, 'Yes, yes,' I would eat, but if the answer was, 'No, no,' I would send it back."[137]

As he remained sick, he decided to adopt a different strategy. Instead of just lying on his mat, he decided to get down on his knees and pray for his recovery. As Jake told Dr. Watson:

I went down on my knees in front of the door, folded my hands to pray, and I really did pray. The first guard came by, beat on the door with his sword, and hollered at me to get back on my bench. It was against the rules for any prisoner even to look at the door. Japanese prisoners received a beating for such audacity, but I did not move when the guard shouted. I felt no fear since God had shown me what to do. I felt a great weight of joy.

In a very short time, the guard returned with several other guards. The door opened and the guards walked into my cell. They never hit me nor hollered at me. They acted a little awed. A medical man came to the cell, and I was picked up and laid down on a straw mat. The medical man rolled up my shirt sleeve and shot some medicine into my arm after which I was left alone in my cell to thank Jesus who was close by my side.

When meal time came, I was surprised to receive a nice pint of milk, boiled eggs, some good well-made bread, and some nice nourishing soup. I couldn't help crying and laughing when I thought how beautifully and wonderfully God had worked this all out for me. From that time until we were released from prison, I received milk, eggs, bread, and good nourishing food. I stayed in bed because I thought that God had indicated that this was the best thing for me to do.[138]

Aside from his conversion, this experience was memorable for Jake. He knew that God's presence was with him in that prison cell. Indeed, it was God who reached out to Him during his time in solitary confinement. Now, God was breathing into Jake a new spiritual life, one that he did not know existed. It was this spiritual rebirth that helped Jake sustain his health. In fact, he had no fear, because he was with God.

On August 10, 1945, he had another experience. Upon waking up, he felt compelled to pray. God's Holy Spirit was beckoning Jake to get down on his knees:

I asked, "What shall I pray about?" "Pray for peace, and pray without ceasing," I was told. I had prayed about peace, but very little if at all before that time, as it seemed useless. I thought God could stop the war any time with His power, which He had manifested.

But God was now teaching me the lesson of cooperation. It was God's joy for me to be willing to let Him use me. God does use human instruments to accomplish His will here on earth. It will be a great joy to us through all eternity if we can cooperate with Him. I started to pray for peace although I had a very poor idea of what was taking place in the world at that time.

I began to pray at about seven o'clock in the morning. It seemed very easy to pray on the subject of peace. I prayed that God would put a great desire in the hearts of the Japanese leaders for peace. I thought about the days of peace that would follow. Japanese people would no doubt be discouraged, and I felt sympathetic toward them. I prayed that God would not allow them to fall into persecution by the victorious armies.

At two o'clock in the afternoon, the Holy Spirit told me, "You don't need to pray any more. The victory is won." I was amazed. I thought this was quicker and better than the regular method of receiving world news. Probably this news broadcast had not come over the radio to America as yet. I thought I would just wait and see what was to happen.[139]

While Jake had no radio, he had experienced a divine revelation. Although he did not realize the significance of what he was told, he learned later that his experience occurred on August 6, 1945, which was the day the first atomic weapon detonated over Hiroshima. DeShazer believed that God had been teaching him. He took from this experience a simple lesson: God wants human beings to pray and that God hears and answers those prayers.

The following days in the prison profoundly affected Jake. He says that he felt the love of God flooding his soul. Day and night he experienced a rapturous joy and he felt as though he was having a foretaste of heaven.[140] Lying on the straw mat, Jake felt spiritually rejuvenated despite his weakened physical state. On that straw mat, he decided to make a promise to God, "I promised God that I would make restitution for the things that I had stolen. I felt certain that I would be able to return to the United States. I was going to make amends as far as God showed me it was the right thing to do. It was a wonderful feeling not to harbor any resentment or ill will toward any one. I felt love toward the Japanese people and a deep interest in their welfare. I felt that we were all made by the same God and that we must share our hardships and our happiness together. How I wished that I could tell the Japanese people about Jesus!"[141]

Jake also wondered what would happen to Japan after the end of the war. Their hopes of victory had been shattered. He couldn't help but feel sorry for the Japanese people. He wondered if the Japanese would be receptive to the Christian message. Jake thought that if the Japanese learned about Jesus, the military defeat to them would turn into a great victory.[142] At this moment, Jake received his calling. The Holy Spirit spoke to him, saying, "You are called to go and teach the Japanese people and to go wherever I send you."[143]

It was hard for Jake to comprehend such a task. To go and minister to the country that harbored him as a prisoner was indeed a test of his Christian faith. Jake knew that this would take hard work and preparation. He began to think about his shortcomings: he was not a good public speaker, he had not attended college, and he lacked training in Christian theology and the Bible. Though his weaknesses were many, he recalled a line in the Lord's Prayer, "Let thy will be done" and realized that he had promised God that he would do His will. Jake thought that at the very least he could be a janitor in some church, but God's voice was pushing him to "Get in and work for all you are worth. You have as good a chance as anyone else."[144] Jake knew that if he had faith as small as a mustard seed that he would succeed in his noble endeavor.

Chapter 10

THE SWEET TASTE OF FREEDOM

Do not snatch the word of truth from my mouth,
for I have put my hope in your laws. I will always
obey your law, for ever and ever. I will walk about
in freedom, for I have sought out your precepts.
—*Psalm 119:43–45*

ON AUGUST 20, 1945, freedom came for Jake DeShazer and the
three other men—a mere ten days after Jake fervently prayed for
peace. Forty months of living in prisons and solitary confinement came to an end. A Japanese officer announced, "The war is over.
You can go home now." The men were elated. They came out of their cells
eager to see one another.

Immediately, they noticed that one man was missing, Lieutenant Barr.
At first, the group thought that Lieutenant Barr had died in prison. A few
minutes later, Lieutenant Barr was helped out of his cell by two Japanese
guards, as he had been very ill.[145] Barr looked frail and his deeply set eyes
spoke volumes about the American's experience in the prison.

The Japanese guards offered to give the Americans a haircut. The men
refused because they did not want to return to the U.S. with a prisoner's
haircut. Their army uniforms, now more than three years old, were returned to them. They were then taken by truck to a large English hotel.
Jake remembered, "Everyone came to look at us, and some tried to tell us
the news. So many things were happening so fast I couldn't seem to keep
up with everything. After someone talked, I couldn't remember what he
had said. My mind wasn't working right."[146]

Although they were eating well at the end of their imprisonment, the
food at the hotel was in a class of its own. They were given as much Irish
stew as they could eat. The doctors also ordered the men to receive vitamin shots. Out among other people they learned of the end of the war, the

dropping of the atomic bomb, and that American paratroopers had flown in to rescue them. The parachute rescue group had journeyed all the way to Peking asking where the Americans were—and the Japanese stated that they had all been executed. However, the rescue group knew this not to be true and put pressure on the Japanese. The Japanese finally cooperated with the rescue group and released the four Doolittle flyers.

But, how did they know that the men were still alive? The story goes that there were ten U.S. Marines who had been imprisoned early in the war at the prison in Nanking. While in prison, some soup was brought to the prisoners in aluminum teacups. One day, Lieutenant Nielsen, while writing numbers on the bottom of one of the cups, noticed that the cup said, "U.S. Marines." Lieutenant Nielsen told the men about it, so when they were out in the yard, they picked up some nails, and sharpened them on the walls of their cells and began writing on the bottom of the cups, and began corresponding with the Marines. This was not noticed for more than two months. During this time, the word got out to the Marines that four Doolittle flyers were in prison.

The ten Marines who were in prison were captured at the very start of the war. After months in the concentration camp, the Marines hatched an escape plan. Ten men tried to flee, but only three escaped. The unlucky seven were put in prison near the Doolittle men and were subjected to severe punishment. At the end of the war, the Marines had been released first and told the American rescue team that there were four Doolittle flyers still in the prison. Armed with this knowledge, the rescue team put pressure on the Japanese until they released the four men.

Once released, the men still needed time to assimilate. When they were given food, they hoarded it for later, just in case they got hungry. Jake recalled, "We would take the food we couldn't eat and store it away in case we became hungry before mealtime. It seemed the natural thing to do. But after a while, some of the people would laugh and ask us if we were getting ready for another famine. It seemed hard to realize that we were free and would not need to suffer from hunger pangs any more."[147]

Another incident involving food happened on the second day after their release. An American woman wanting to do something to help came to visit the men. She had been living in Peking with her French business-man husband since before the war, "She asked us what we would like. The other fellows asked me to say, so I told the lady that I could not think of a better thing than ice cream. She said that is what we would get and she would make it herself. The next day, we ate a freezer full of ice cream, which was a real treat to us."[148]

Three days after their release, all of the flyers, except for Lieutenant Barr due to health reasons, were flown to Chungking to begin their voyage home. News of their release on August 20 was heard around the world. Families finally knew, after forty long months, the fate of their sons. Jake's family was elated upon hearing the news. His mother, who had prayed and prayed for her son, was full of joy. She seemed to be doubly blessed with the news that her son was alive and had become a Christian while in prison, having decided to give the rest of his life to missionary work. In his oral history, Jake recounted that, "Mother received the news through a telegram relayed from her former farm home at Madras to her telephone-less home in Salem. 'It's wonderful, of course,' she exclaimed, 'but I keep thinking how terrible it is for the other mothers whose sons weren't rescued.'"[149]

Pictures of Jake on his knees were in many newspapers. Many thought he was just seeking the limelight, while others thought he meant well, but it was only a short-lived idea. The families of the other men, including Lieutenants Hallmark, Farrow, Meder, and Sergeant Spatz, learned the heartbreaking fate of their loved ones.

The men made it home by way of India and across the Atlantic. De-Shazer sent word to his parents from Washington D.C., where he reiterated the story of his conversion and his desire to return to Japan as a missionary. While in Washington, the men were taken to Walter Reed Medical Hospital to be examined.

When they arrived at Walter Reed, Major General Shelley Marietta and the medical staff greeted them. They were immediately given a rehabilitation program designed to mitigate the negative effects of their time in prison and solitary confinement. The former prisoners told the doctors how they had been beaten and threatened with death by their captors. The flyers then underwent a series of physical checkups. Upon examination, doctors discovered that the men lost an average of thirty pounds each. The first treatment prescribed by the doctors was food. Their first meal consisted of tenderloin steak, fried chicken, and milk. Of all the items served that day, the men loved that cold glass of milk the most since, for some, it was the first one they had had since leaving the *Hornet* for the mission. After dinner, they were issued new uniforms, with awards and decorations and were promoted three grades.[150]

As would be expected, the former prisoners were subjected to many interviews from the press. Various newspapers offered them money for one quote. Jake received four hundred dollars just for reading one sentence over the radio. He later told Dr. Watson that it was the most that he had ever been paid for opening his mouth.[151] He received $2,250 from a newspaper to recount his personal story. He also received the $5,600 in back pay for the forty months he had been in prison. Despite the attention, Jake longed to go home and get on with life.

He also began to experience the degree to which the press distorted his words. In a letter to his mother, he noted, "I'm not sure when I'm coming home. I hope you don't believe everything the papers say, I am not bitter toward the Japs...and I don't think the officers are either. We feel sorry for them. They don't know any better way to live. Sometimes they treated us very good."[152] Indeed, the papers had a hard time getting their stories right.[153] The Associated Press in particular published statements that the men simply did not say.

To prevent the release of stories that were not factually accurate or flat-out fabricated, the men made a contract with one company, the Inter national News Service (INS). The men signed a contract to tell their story to them exclusively. For this, the INS paid them well. After sitting down for a few hours with an INS reporter, Jake notes that their full story would be published in a week's time.

In his letters home, Jake also began to talk about his desire for an education, specifically a missionary's education. Jake told his mother, "I want to go to a missionary school and learn to preach to the Japs."[154] He fervently believed that God had given him a message, one he had "written down now" and that it was his destiny to fulfill it. While Jake had no formal theological training, he possessed a powerful personal faith and had had a remarkable conversion experience. These two personal qualities would be supplemented greatly by a college education. He concluded that all that he needed now was the knowledge and confidence to proclaim this message to a country he believed was in need of the healing power of Jesus Christ.[155]

Jake's correspondence to his family recounted the story that would be the hallmark of his future career—his time in solitary confinement. He shared with his mother how in the thirty-four months of isolation, he became a new person. God had healed him from sickness, told him what to eat, taught him how to pray, and gave him knowledge of the war's end.[156] Jake thought his story would be one that would bring people to

God. Indeed, his story would stir the hearts and souls of many, both at home and abroad.

The story of Jake's conversion immediately began to resonate with many Americans. One of the people affected was army Chaplain Perry O. Wilcox. In a letter written by Perry to Jake's mother, he said:

> Dear Ms. Andrus:
>
> One of the most important things that I have seen in the news recently is a news item concerning your son, Staff Sergeant Jacob D. DeShazer, who states that he has a conviction that the answer to the Japanese situation is to be found in the doctrine of Jesus of Nazareth.
>
> In 1901, John R. Mott made the statement, "America will send ten thousand missionaries to Japan now, or in forty years, they will send one hundred thousand rifles." He was right, except that we sent one hundred times the rifles as he counted on. I believe that unless we can succeed in establishing something other than hate in the hearts of humanity, the chance of permanent world peace is very slim.
>
> I congratulate you on having such a son.
>
> Most sincerely yours,
>
> Perry O. Wilcox[157]

Other letters similar to this would come in Jake's lifetime. In the meanwhile, Jake was still trying to figure out how to best achieve his plan to become a missionary. While on the plane ride to the West Coast from Washington D.C., Jake assessed his life. He recalled his days as a youth and in the army, with the idleness, drinking, smoking, and gambling. He was not proud of them. Becoming a minister meant that one had to be above the vices and vicissitudes of everyday life. How could his ministry glorify and exemplify Christ if Jake himself was not striving to live a Christlike life? At that moment, he was compelled by God to vow to never again touch alcohol or tobacco. He did not want these potential distractions to get in the way of his ministry. Jake felt a desire to get busy with the work that God had called him to do.[158]

Upon arriving home, his family and friends were elated. Prayers had been offered every day and night for his safe return. They gathered again, this time with Jake in their midst, and offered prayers of thanksgiving. The family knew that Jake had become a changed person. In his youth, he rebelled against his family's ardent faith in God and the Bible. Now, Jake was a believer and wanted to pray with his family. At one particular instance, Jake, his family, and a close friend, Mrs. J. R. Stewart, were on their knees giving thanks to God. People spoke their prayers aloud. Jake was moved by their beautiful words and when they had finished he tried to pray like they did. Though he tried to formulate his intense emotions into prayer, nothing came out. Jake was frustrated. He had the desire, the faith, and the will to pray, but his faculties did not respond. After the prayer service, Jake told the others that he wished to pray aloud as they had done. Everyone was supportive saying that this would come in time.[159]

While all his family was happy to see him, his mother was particularly glad. Jake was still thin and his mother was determined to remedy this. Hulda cooked Jake's favorite meal, fried chicken. Jake ate all the food he wanted and more. Milk, cake, chicken, beef, and other delicious goodies helped Jake gain an average of one pound a day for the twenty days he was at home.[160]

When he had gained enough strength, Jake journeyed to his hometown of Madras and a great celebration was held in his honor. While in Madras, he gave a speech about his being in prison and his conversion. This was the first of many speeches he would give throughout his life. As Jake notes, "It was a good place to begin my speechmaking, so I told as much as I could remember about the prison and about the salvation I had received when I read the Bible. I ran out of wind pretty fast. I was sweating and working harder than I had ever in my life. It seems funny now, but I was nearly thirty-three years old, and this was my first public speech. In bed alone that night, I prayed to God. I felt comfort from Him and a promise of victory if I would continue to try."[161] In addition to this, Jake gave two additional speeches, one at a local evangelical church, and the other in the presence of Dr. Nathan Cohen Beskin, a converted Russian Jew.[162] Making speeches became a bit easier, but he had much room for improvement. Telling his story only strengthened his resolve to polish his public speaking skills and go to college.

Jake was supposed to have an uninterrupted ninety-day leave from the army. However, his leave was cut short when he was asked for some unknown reason to report to Santa Ana Air Base in California only two weeks after arriving home. After arriving at Santa Ana, he asked to be discharged from the army. To his surprise, they informed him that this was impossible for some time because there were so many soldiers who were to be discharged. Not having much to do, he visited much of Santa Ana. Having several relatives in the area, he was then invited to speak at churches and youth services. The crowds loved hearing Jake's story and enjoyed interacting with him. At one church, a member asked Jake if he had ever been baptized. Jake responded that a blustery rain shower had baptized him in his prison cell. He recalled this experience with great joy and the audience was captivated by Jake's faith and sincerity.

During his time in Santa Ana, a leading military official committed a major blunder involving some fifty former POWs. These fifty POWs, including Jake, were told to report for KP duty. Jake was still recovering from scabies and should have been resting, but instead he was put on KP duty.[163]

Jake was made to clean dishes at a mess hall. One day, while carrying out his duties, a newspaper reporter came in and without authorization took Jake's picture. There followed quite the uproar when the photograph circulated depicting a weak and emaciated Jake carrying large heavy trays of dirty dishes. The picture appeared in one of the leading Los Angeles newspapers under the title "War Prisoners Return: Put on Army KP Duty." In the article, an officer said that there was no discrimination between duties as the men waited to be discharged: "We're awfully short-handed and somebody has to stand KP. It probably will only happen to them once or twice while they are here."[164]

When the public saw this, there was an outcry and backlash against the military authorities for putting Jake and other POWs in the positions to carry out such menial tasks. The officials responsible were given a reprimand. DeShazer was sent immediately to a hospital for further observation and care. This incident also resulted in an intensified effort to give Jake his requested discharge. Just prior to being sent to the hospital, he was called in to see the commanding officer who admitted it had been a great mistake for him to have been out on KP duty, and that he would do everything possible to help.

Jake—on farm in Madras,
Oregon

Jake—high school annual, 1931

Jake—Army Air Corps portrait, 2/26/40

The *Bat's* crew, shortly before the Doolittle Raid:
Barr, Farrow, Spatz, Hite, and DeShazer

B-25 takeoff—4/18/42

Jake—two weeks after release from
POW camp, August 1945

Jake—1945

Jake—arriving home, 9/18/45

Florence Matheny—1945

Jake—1946

Jake and Florence—wedding day, 8/29/46

Jake and Florence—sailing for Japan,
12/14/48

Jake and Florence—with the Yoshiki family,
Winter 1948

Jake—after his first sermon, 1/2/49

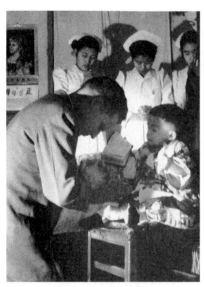

Jake—praying over a sick child at a hospital

Rev. Kaneo Oda—1949

Jake and Rev. Oda—preaching to a gathering, 1949

Jake and Florence—with John and Paul, Summer 1950

Jake and Florence—with Paul and John and the Aota family
(former POW prison guard), 1950

Jake—his car with loudspeakers mounted on the
roof, 1952

Jake and Fuchida—on Fuchida's baptism
day, Spring 1952

Jake and Florence—with their five children, 1959

Jake and Florence—with Nagoya church group, 1960

Jake and Florence—with three of their children, street evangelism in Nagoya farm region, 1963

Jake and his POW companions—Nielsen, Hite, and Barr,
reunion in Los Angeles

Jake—preaching in Japan, 1975

Jake—signing autographs at Raider's reunion, April 1998

Jake—with Hite, Hamada, and Nielsen, at the *Pearl Harbor* premier in Hawaii, 5/20/01

Jake—the sixtieth Raiders reunion with his silver goblet, April 2002

Jake and the author—Carol Aiko with her Dad, 2004

Jake and Florence—Salem, Oregon, 3/29/04

Chapter 11

THE QUEST FOR KNOWLEDGE:
LIFE AS A STUDENT AT
SEATTLE PACIFIC COLLEGE

*Instruct a wise man and he will be wiser still; teach
a righteous man and he will add to his learning.*
—Proverbs 9:9

O N HIS WAY home, Jake stopped by Seattle Pacific College (now
Seattle Pacific University) to visit his sister Helen. Helen was
studying and working as a secretary in the office for Dr. Watson,
the president of S.P.C. Helen knew about Jake's college ambitions. She also
knew that, since his return, he had been bombarded with literature and
catalogs from dozens of colleges and universities across the U.S. Helen
believed Jake would be an ideal fit at S.P.C. She told Dr. Watson, "I am
hoping that S.P.C. will be his [Jake's] choice of a college, but we will be
happy with whatever decision he makes."[165] She later encouraged Watson
to send Jake a blank application to prompt him to apply.[166] On September
20, the president penned a personal note to Jake:

Dear Jacob:

I trust you will allow me to address you by your
first name; since Helen has been my secretary this
summer, I have come to feel very close to you. I am
sure God now has a plan whereby you can use the
tragic experiences of the last forty months for the
uplift and salvation of many. We pray God's blessing
upon you as you go forward in fellowship with the
Lord. I have just received a card from Helen indi-

cating your desire for an application blank from the
school. She indicated you were anxious to get started
immediately with your school program. Be assured of
our willingness and desire to cooperate in every way.
If possible, it would be splendid for you to be here by
Friday morning, September 28. The program of that
day and of Saturday, the 29th, will make it possible
for our teachers to give you better advice in regard to
enrollment.[167]

Jake felt overwhelmed. He had not yet been discharged from the army
and he was already receiving applications from many good schools. He
also received calls to speak all over the West Coast. One speaking engagement came from the church of Reverend Finkbeiner in North Central
Washington at Okanogan, who had been a friend of Jake's. He accepted
the invitation and also decided to stop by S.P.C. to visit Helen.

When Jake arrived, he not only saw his sister, but he also met Dr.
Watson. Jake sat down to discuss his future plans with him and noted,
"Watson asked me when I was going to start school. I said I didn't think
I could go to school before the winter quarter, but he gave me a good
chance to start immediately if I so desired. The result was that the next
day I started to college."[168] Helen believed that President Watson made a
favorable impression on Jake since Jake decided to enroll at S.P.C. just a
day after his visit.

Everything was happening so quickly for Jake. Just two months after
being released from prison, he was to become a student. Thoughts of doubt
began to race through his head. How would he adjust to the rigors of college academics? Should he have taken more time to rest? Would he be able
to meet the requirements to become a missionary? Would a man in his
early thirties make friends with a younger group of students? Reflecting
on all that was happening Jake decided, "Think of it! Only three months
before the time I started to school I had been seriously ill and thought I
was going to die. God had healed me from sickness, baptized me with the
Holy Spirit, and provided everything I needed to prepare me to become
a missionary. How impossible it had all seemed to me, but all God asked
me to do was to try, and then He worked. The government was paying all
of my tuition and was giving me subsistence money. I was free to give my
full time to study. I felt as if God had brought me to school."[169] Despite

the fact that Jake had not been in school for many years, and had not read much other than the Bible in prison, he had a thirst for knowledge and was determined to work hard to accomplish his goal.

At S.P.C., Jake was able to surround himself in an environment that reinforced his Christian faith. He also found a faculty dedicated to the study of Christian Theology and the Bible, which would help transform Jake into a competent missionary.

The change from prison life to a college campus was dramatic. In prison, Jake was beaten, berated, and humiliated. He had little time for himself and was forced to do menial chores. At S.P.C., he had the freedom of personal activity and free inquiry. He could attend classes, study, and partake in extracurricular activities among other things. It was astonishing to think that just three months earlier he had been a POW. Now, he was at a place that was helping him assimilate back into society while at the same time cultivating his spiritual being.

Seattle Pacific College is nestled in the Queen Anne area of suburban Seattle. A few blocks from the campus was a gorgeous view of downtown Seattle and the bay. Jake found the environment at S.P.C. both aesthetically pleasing and personally inviting. At S.P.C., he became a typical student. According to Jake, "I was staying at the men's residence hall...I was older than most of them, but no one seemed to notice...The young people at S.P.C. were the finest people with whom I had ever associated. After my war experience, I felt as if I had come in from a howling wind storm into a good strong house...I could see living examples of what the Holy Spirit taught me in prison."[170]

Jake also sang the praises of S.P.C.'s faculty members. He notes that they were "Spirit-filled. They knew the Bible. They could give splendid instruction and wise counsel. I never realized before coming to this college that God had so many people who were so nearly perfect in their lives. They had the same idea that God had given me."[171] Jake threw himself into his classes and was anxious to learn. In his mind, he was constantly comparing the instruction he was given to his experience in prison. Jake found compatibility between the two. The lectures by his professors gave him a depth of knowledge that helped him better formulate his thoughts and ideas. Jake notes that his teachers "encouraged us in every means of grace available, such as singing songs, reading the Bible, giving testimonies, memorizing Scripture, praying, and associating with other Christians."[172]

Although this was supposed to be a time dedicated to learning, Jake found himself being called to speak so frequently that it almost derailed his studies. Indeed, requests came from far and wide to have him come and talk about his prison experience and give his testimony. The sheer volume of requests began to overwhelm Jake. In order to alleviate this stress, S.P.C. assigned the Reverend George T. Klein to try to manage Jake's schedule. They worked together to create a leaflet highlighting Jake's story. This gave Jake more time to focus on his schoolwork since he did not have to write a new speech or presentation each time he went to speak. Still, Jake and Rev. Klein made an average of three trips a week where Jake was the key speaker.[173]

It was during this period that he began to associate with the Free Methodist Church (F.M.C.). His parents had been members of the F.M.C. for years, but now Jake felt it was time for him to formally belong to the denomination. The most important aspect of the F.M.C. was that it was rooted firmly in the Bible. The Bible was held as the inviolate Word of God and was the cornerstone of one's faith in Christ. The church advocated one to seek complete separation from sin and to live a Spirit-filled life. The F.M.C. also had a practical impact on Jake's life as it recognized his desire to be a missionary. To that end, the church granted him a local preacher's license, which was his first step toward becoming an ordained minister.[174]

Jake's school experiences were like night and day when compared with the forty months of internment he endured. He notes, "Everyone on campus called me 'Jake.' It seemed that they all knew me since my name and pictures had been in the papers. I tried to remember the other students' names, but it seemed difficult…however, they were all my friends, and I enjoyed their friendship very much."[175] Things were going well for him at S.P.C. Unlike his sister, Helen, Jake did not have to work for an income while attending S.P.C. In fact, he was fairly well-off as a result of his military subsistence check. This source of income enabled him, unlike many other students at the time, to purchase an automobile. Soon after, he began ferrying students back and forth to services off-campus—especially if he was to speak. His funds also allowed him to support student prayer activities on campus, which only heightened his reputation as an all-around good person. Indeed, his life had made an unexpected turn for the better.

As Jake's first year of college came to a close, he made plans to continue his studies in the summer term. He felt as though God was calling him to press on through his degree. So determined was Jake that he decided to try and complete a four-year college degree in three calendar years. While his income made this financially possible, another incentive came along in the form of a lovely Christian woman named Miss Florence Matheny.

Chapter 12

The Meeting, Courtship, and Marriage of Florence Matheny to Jacob DeShazer

Then the LORD God made a woman from the rib he had
taken out of the man, and he brought her to the man. The
man said, "This is now bone of my bones and flesh of my
flesh; she shall be called 'woman,' for she was taken out of
man." For this reason a man will leave his father and mother
and be united to his wife, and they will become one flesh.
—*Genesis 2:22-24*

FLORENCE FAYE MATHENY was born on August 9, 1921, in the town
of Toddville, Iowa. Her dad, Archie Mathney, was a farmer who
had an avid love of music and would often sing at the local PTA
and Farm Bureau meetings. Archie played the violin, trumpet, fife, juice-
harp, and harmonica. Her mother, Alice, was a quiet and deeply spiritual
person. Florence recalls that her favorite memory of her mother is of seeing her kneeling at the floor of her bed in a white nightgown. Florence
thought that her mother was praying for the health and safety of her
children.

Florence had an older sister named Margaret. She developed juvenile
diabetes when she turned five years old. Because of this, Margaret never
was able to eat the things that typical kids ate such as ice cream, cake, and
other sweets. Margaret and Florence were close and developed a strong
relationship. The sisters took care of their brother, Archie Jr., who was ten
years younger than Florence. They would often change Archie's diapers
and would take turns giving him a bottle of warm milk. Florence had
a younger sister named Phyllis who was born in 1932, eleven years after
Florence. Like her sister, Phyllis loved music and sports.

Florence grew up on a farm and attended the Little Head Country School before entering high school. She took an active role in her family, mainly as a caregiver to her siblings. Phyllis remembers how Florence would read aloud to her and her brother. When Florence was reading a story, she would often stop at the end of the chapter to give her brother and sister a chance to guess what would happen next.[176] Florence would also help her mother in organizing and cleaning of the house.

She enjoyed sports and the competition that they brought. She was a member of the basketball team, which in 1936 won the Linn County championship. Her love of sports would stay with her for the rest of her life.

The other activity that accompanied young Florence's childhood was church. She enjoyed the visits of the missionaries that would visit her church after spending time in far off locations.[177] Like many of the children raised in Christian homes, she attended Sunday school where she learned about the Bible and Jesus Christ. However, like her future husband, her faith did not play a central role in her life at that time.

At thirteen years of age, Florence entered the Monroe Township High School at Toddville. She did well there academically as she graduated in 1938 with a 3.00 grade point average. After high school, she wanted to become a teacher. To achieve this goal, Florence had to leave the little town of Toddville and attended Lenox Junior College at Hopkinton, Iowa, in the fall of 1938.

Life as a college student kept Florence busy and she had little time for her faith. She had the typical distractions of homework, sports, and a few dates. Florence admitted that her mother's prayers helped her to keep on the straight and narrow path as she tried to balance her time.[178] She remembers that her "heart was black" because she was not then a Christian.[179]

In 1939, she entered her sophomore year. Determined to become a school teacher, she had to take courses that were required for her teaching certification. It was during that time that Florence began to realize that she was missing a spiritual dimension in her life. She had read the gospel in church and had various opportunities to accept the mercy extended by Jesus, but she said no to these invitations.[180] There were numerous times when she was on the verge of opening her heart to Christ, but she continued to withdraw. Her reluctance stemmed from the thought of having to break friendships with friends who were non-Christians.

On June 2, 1940, she graduated from junior college receiving her diploma and completing the requirements for her teaching certification. Her first job began in August 1940, which was in her hometown in a rural school. Being back in a familiar place meant that she was once again attending church services and was in the company of many Christian families. After teaching for a few months, she became a secretary at her local church. She continued in this position for a whole year.

In August 1941, a new pastor came to the church. The pastor and his wife took an interest in young Florence. Florence liked the pastor since he was amiable and outgoing. One evening, the pastor suggested that Florence attend a talk featuring a leading figure in the evangelism community. Florence, along with several other young people, attended. When they arrived to hear the gentleman, they found the church filled as people were packed in the pews. The only seats available were in the front row.

The speaker gave a powerful sermon about the transformative power of God, which seemed to have a great impact on the audience. After the speech, there was an altar call for those seeking to accept the Lord. As the altar filled with people, Florence brushed aside the feelings she had. Her cynical nature prevented her from going up to the altar.

As she stood in the church watching the people pass her, she heard a voice address her saying, "Wouldn't you like to be a Christian?"[181] She recognized the voice as it was her pastor's. The appeal on his face and the urgency in his voice disarmed Florence. At that moment, she heard the voice of Christ say, "Come unto me and I will give you rest."[182] The voice echoed in her head and opened her eyes to the realization that she needed God's saving love and grace in her life. Overwhelmed by the moment, she fell to her knees and began to pray. She remembers trying to make "an honest effort to pray, but no words came."[183] Although unable to pray, she remembered Psalm 51:15, which states that "a broken and contrite heart, O God, thou wilt not despise" (KJV). At that moment, Florence welcomed the love of Christ into her heart. When she got up off her knees, she felt as though the weight of sin was gone and she was happy that she had decided to follow Jesus "no matter the cost."[184] The decision to follow Christ was one of the most important in her life.

For the next three years, Florence continued working as a secretary and Sunday school teacher at her church. During these years, Florence prayed for wisdom and discernment in regard to a future vocation. Her prayers were answered in the summer of 1945. At a tent meeting one evening, she felt that the Lord wanted her to go into missionary service. Such a calling was noble indeed! She had been enthralled by the stories she heard from missionaries who came to speak at her church. This was a life of adventure and great importance as she would be the bringer of the Good News to non-Christians.

She also felt that in a small town like hers, the possibility of finding a marriage partner with the shared calling to missions was next to impossible. This became a double calling for Florence—one, to go to the mission field, and the other to live a single life. She believed that she was probably giving up the idea of ever having a marriage partner. So, her path seemed crystal clear. She would leave her job as a secretary and teacher, separate herself from her family, friends, and hometown, and enter college. Once finished with college, she would lead the life of a single missionary dedicated to spreading God's Word. After conducting some research, she decided that Seattle Pacific College was the school that would best prepare her for a life as a missionary.

After making the decision to go to college, Florence had an unusual experience. By chance she picked up a newspaper and saw a picture of one of Jimmy Doolittle's flyers that had recently been released after forty months in a Japanese prison camp. She saw a photo of Jacob DeShazer eating his mother's fried chicken. She read the rest of Jacob's story with interest. She learned how he came to Christianity while in solitary confinement and how his newfound faith gave him the strength and fortitude to endure the years in prison. Perhaps what most impressed Florence was DeShazer's commitment to return to Japan to preach the gospel. The article mentioned that DeShazer planned on attending a Christian college located in the U.S. Ruminating on this, Florence thought, "What a coincidence it would be if he should choose the same college I've chosen. Perhaps I might even get to shake hands with him. Who knows?"[185]

The trip to Seattle Pacific College was a big adventure. It was the first time she had traveled outside of Iowa. In that journey, she witnessed a new landscape filled with mountains and she would later see the ocean. In order to get to Seattle, Florence had to ride in a car with the former pastor J. K. French of the Toddsville Free Methodist Church and his family, who happened to be moving to Oregon.

She mailed many letters to her family in Iowa during her travels westward. Her letters were vivid in imagery and details as she described in detail what she saw. She was hoping to convey to her family the new and wondrous scenery she was seeing. Florence was particularly moved when she saw the ocean. In a letter she said, "[Y]ou can't realize what the ocean is like until you actually see it. It is just water, water, water, as far as you can see. And huge waves come rolling in one after another. We all took our shoes and stockings off and waded in. It sure was fun."[186]

In today's world of instant communication, it is hard to understand that the only way of staying in touch with one's family was to write letters. In the twenty-first century, there are cell phones, e-mail, text messages, and instant messages. Even if family members live at opposite ends of the country, they are never out of reach. Florence, however, did not have the option to pick up a telephone or send her family e-mails. She communicated with her family through her letters. She would write each member of her family individually, sometimes concerning the same subject, but it was her way of maintaining their close family ties.

In her letters, she asked many questions about home, especially on the topics of sports. She wanted to know how her brother's baseball team was doing, what kind of movies were playing, if they had popcorn when they went to the movies, and what kind of grades her siblings were receiving. She wrote about how she missed her church and spending time canning food with her mother. For Florence, writing was not only a way to keep in touch with her family, but also a way for her to process new experiences. To this end, she would write her family often more than once a day in her journey to Washington State. She, no doubt, felt a bit alone in her travels. Here she was, a young women traveling to attend college in a new place. In order to combat this feeling of aloneness, she would always end her letters, "Don't forget to write."

After a week of travel, Florence arrived at S.P.C. on September 25, 1945. She liked the campus as it was nestled in the hills of the Queen Anne district in Seattle. She also enjoyed the weather. At this time, the mild summer temperatures were giving way to a cooler fall. In the opening convocation ceremony, Florence heard S.P.C. president Watson speak. In his opening remarks, he talked glowingly about the students and the college. He said that was going to be the biggest class for the school in its history with more than six hundred students enrolling. Dr. Watson was proud to announce that S.P.C. was also welcoming two hundred veterans to its campus.

In order to deal with the increase in students, sixteen new faculty members had been added. Additionally, Watson discussed how the college had converted the former military barracks into new classrooms and laboratories. He also mentioned the opening of Watson Hall, a dormitory for women complete with individual bathrooms and a cafeteria.

After the ceremony, Florence left to find her dorm room, which was located in Alexander Hall. When she saw the room, she was not happy with it so she asked if she could be transferred to another one. There was one room located on the fourth floor and she decided that she would take that one because it was "the very nicest one in the dorm."[187] In room 405, Florence met her new roommate, Lois. Florence wrote her mother, "She sure is a nice roommate. She is a fine Christian and likes most of the same things I do."[188]

The first few weeks of college were exciting. The school kept Florence busy with activities such as movie showings, campus-sponsored parties, and chapel services that allowed the students to get acquainted with one another. Florence attended all of these, which helped her adjust to college life. She had a busy academic schedule and wrote to her sister that she was taking a full course load, which included Speech, Physical Education, Christian Education of Children, Educational Psychology, and Character Education. In addition to classes, Florence worked fourteen hours a week for sixty-five cents an hour, making a bit more than nine dollars a week. This paid for clothes, supplies, and other college expenses.

In her trips around Seattle, she did not forget to send her family souvenirs. She also described attending a Youth for Christ rally in a large theater building in downtown Seattle. She was moved by the whole event. She claimed that there were more than fifteen thousand people there and that many came up to the altar to accept Christ.

Florence was fitting in well at S.P.C. and really liked her classmates, "Everyone here is so nice, at least 90 percent of the students are Christians, and it is really wonderful to be in a group like that."[189]

In a letter to Phyllis, Florence noted a new development that was buzzing around S.P.C.'s campus. She told her sister that Jake DeShazer, a former Doolittle raider, was supposed to be attending S.P.C. next quarter. This was the second time that Florence mentioned Jake. In the first letter, she wrote about what an honor it would be to shake his hand and perhaps this would come true.

As college life settled down, Florence was busy studying for exams, playing volleyball, and working. Letters home while consistent were less frequent, because she balanced her time between work, classes, rallies, and sports. In a letter to her mother in October 1945, she wrote that she was sorry for not writing for four days because she was caught up in other things, like taking tests in educational psychology.[190] She sometimes felt a bit slighted because family members had not written to her in a "timely manner." In one letter to her brother she wrote, "It's been a long time since I wrote you, hasn't it? But not so long as it has been since you have written to me. Is all your time taken up with Betty? Or do you suppose you could spend a little time to drop me a postcard at least? I want to know all about your ball games, parties, grades, etc...now please write and tell me all this stuff."[191]

In November 1945, Florence wrote her family that her classes were getting busy. She was trying to get work done before going to the Pastor French's house for the Thanksgiving holiday. Despite her schedule, she still managed to play volleyball and noted that her team was 5–0.[192] In a letter to her mother, she also mentioned attending a school fair with Jacob DeShazer, "the famous Doolittle flyer." She was teased by her friends who "have her married off to him and on her way to Japan."[193] What struck Florence about Jake was his story. She mentioned hearing Jake's story in church one Sunday. She said, "It was a very stirring message. He is bashful and modest and it is hard for him to speak in public, but his story is so stirring and unusual that it makes up for any lack of speech technique."[194]

With a potential budding romance with Jake DeShazer, Florence finished her first semester in college. She was glad to have her exams over and believed that she would receive mostly C's in her classes with the exception of an A in gym.[195] As it turned out, Florence did better than expected as she earned two C's, two B's, and an A. She spent Christmas break with the French's and even had the chance to meet and have dinner with Jake's mother. After the break, she returned to S.P.C. where she discovered that tragedy had befallen one of her roommates, Eunice, who was accidentally shot to death while hunting. This was indeed a tragedy, but Florence found comfort in her faith.[196]

In January 1946, things continued to change for Florence and the nation. As more veterans returned home from war, the girls at S.P.C. found themselves losing space to accommodate the influx of servicemen who wanted to attend school on the new GI Bill. Indeed, girls found themselves four to a room. With a change in thinking and union leadership, bus service, newspapers, and telephones went on strike. Florence noted that this would have never happened during the war. Florence was also trying to be frugal. Although she was working, she could not go out and buy the latest clothing. Instead, she only bought what she needed including fabrics, which she sent home to her mother along with her measurements so that her mom could make a skirt for her. She was thrifty throughout her life.

Despite the tough academic load, Florence continued to play sports. She became captain of the class basketball team and wrote of her excitement of the upcoming volleyball season. Florence also enjoyed playing pingpong and tennis with her friends. She relayed one troubling story to her parents, which took place during a tennis match. While she and her friends were playing one evening, Riza, a Russian girl preparing to travel to Russia as a missionary, cut her eye when the ball hit her glasses. The accident caused her to lose one eye. Florence and her friends blamed themselves for the accident. She told her parents that Riza's surgery cost more than two thousand dollars and that Riza still wanted to serve God even after the loss of her eye.[197]

Outside of sports, friends, and classes Florence continued to go out on dates with Jake and other young men. As time went on, she began to write exclusively about Jake. She told the family about riding to Portland in his car. It became apparent that she really liked Jake, saying, "He is sure a swell kid. He has put on some weight and his hair is grown out dark and curly. He is really good looking."[198]

She wrote home and told her sister that Jake asked her out on a date to go to the Youth for Christ Spring Jubilee, "He looked so nice when he picked me up. He had a brand new suit. He looks so much different than when he first came from Japan. Three couples [accompanied] us. Jake has a nice shiny black two seated car with radio and all."[199] The crowd was large with more than eleven thousand people in attendance. She had a good time with Jake and noted that they "were supposed to be back [to the dorm] by eleven that night, but didn't return until midnight. Boy, was our housemother mad."[200]

The more time she spent with Jake, the more she learned about Jake's unique situation. She noted, "It is really something to go out with such an important personage. People are always coming up to him to ask if he is Jake DeShazer and when he says yes, they gush all over him. In spite of all of this attention, he is not 'puffed-up' or conceited."[201]

She and Jake began to spend a lot more time together, almost putting Jake first to her studies as they were always going to rallies. Jake continued to give speeches and his testimony. She wrote to her folks that she was going to Everett with Jake so that he could give his life story. This would be the fifth time that she has heard it, but, as she said, she "still enjoys it."[202] She also believed that she could preach his story since she knew it almost by heart.[203] Although Jake was getting better at delivering his speech and wasn't getting nearly as nervous, Florence believed he still would benefit from more speech training.[204]

Florence stayed at school over the summer to take classes. It gave her an opportunity to progress in her studies and to be close to Jake. Jake was indeed a hot ticket for the college and they kept him busy with speaking engagements and travel. Sometimes he spoke four times or more on Sundays. While her letters used to be full of questions about home, they now consisted of things she and Jake were doing, telling them how wonderful it was in Seattle and that she was alive and able to enjoy it all. While she did miss her family and her hometown, she preferred the climate out west. As for Jake, she said, "I never did dream that I would become so well acquainted with such a distinguished celebrity. He's just a farm kid at heart, though, even if he is thirty-three, he acts like eighteen at times."[205]

It was no surprise, however, that in the next letter home Florence referred to Jake as their future son-in-law, "We have been engaged (but haven't made it pubic) since last Friday night, just five weeks from my first date with him. After a talk at a church, Jake took me out for a ride to Lake Washington where he asked me to be his wife."[206] They both had a similar worldview and were leaving the fate of their future in the Lord's hands. Jake, she said, was different from most Christians, "[b]eing saved in prison like he was he is not bound by convictions and petty prejudices like most of us are. [I]nstead, he preaches the spirit of love. He really lives it, too. I have never seen him slightly irritated at anyone or anything. While in prison, the fellows called him *Job* because he had so much patience."[207]

The preparations for the wedding took place during the summer months. Jake gave Florence an engagement present of a ninety-dollar Swiss-made watch. Throughout the summer they continued to attend rallies and services where Jake continued to hone his speaking skills while giving his life story. Florence began to take a larger role when Jake had a speaking engagement, from shaking hands to sitting on the platform to speaking herself. She wrote, "I am really very happy and know that the Lord has surely led me to Seattle Pacific College and has a great place for us to fill in the future. I feel unworthy and incapable, but know that He is able to help us."[208]

Over the summer they received gifts and money from people in the church. By August they had received about $215 in wedding presents. Helping to defray expenses, they found out that they would also have a house costing them nineteen dollars a month and that Jake would receive ninety dollars a month from the U.S. Government. Additionally, the college would pay all of Jake's traveling expenses when he went to speak on their behalf.

As the days went by, newspaper notices began to appear and refer to Jake as the "Doolittle Flyer" or "Tokyo Raider" and Florence as the "College Girl." Jake bought Florence a piano accordion, which she believed would be useful on the mission field.

The wedding took place in Gresham, Oregon, at the Gresham Free Methodist Church on August 29, 1946. Shortly after, Florence and Jacob traveled to Iowa to see Florence's family. All the while, Jake was busy giving his testimony at churches in Iowa and during the trip back to Seattle. This was just a prelude of Florence's future life with Jake.

Jacob was in the news before marrying Florence. However, Florence had to adjust to the spotlight after she married the "famous Doolittle flyer." As they returned home from Iowa and began to settle into the routine of being newlyweds and students, newspapermen still saw Jacob as a newsworthy item. They took photos of Florence and him doing their daily routines and wrote small articles about them, which continued to appear in the paper touting Jake and Florence and the mission that they were preparing to undertake.

Life for the newlyweds was an extension of what life was like prior to getting married, but now instead of only taking care of herself, Florence had to assume the roles of wife, homemaker, and student. Along with her regular coursework, she and Jake began to take Japanese from Professor Bokko Tsuchiyama in preparation for their mission to Japan.

Married life in postwar America was not all roses. There were shortages of meat, soap, and shortening, and it was hard to make ends meet with the little money they had. They managed to get by on donations of canned goods from friends and family. In the beginning, Jake helped out a great deal in the home.

Florence was elected as the women's athletic director of volleyball. They both were busy with studies, having services and meetings, as well as being appointed prayer leaders. To help Jake with his presentations, the Bible Meditation League created a tract about Jake's life called, *I Was a*

Prisoner of Japan. The tract was printed in more than twenty languages and was sent to churches around the world. Florence wrote of this time, "I have the best husband in the world. We are really happy in the service of the Lord and know that He is guiding and leading our lives."[209]

Throughout their first year of marriage they continued with their studies as well as attending church and revivals to prepare them for their mission work in Japan. This included attending a Japanese Baptist church service where they found that they had difficulty understanding the language. Jake continued preaching and finally was able to take the flying lessons he wanted so long ago. Florence found herself teaching children with object lessons—something she would spend a lot of her life doing. In winter 1947, they sent a preliminary application to the Mission Board to be granted permission to go to Japan.

As life got busier, Florence's letters exhibited a sense of weariness. She wrote, "I am learning more and more that the things of this earth do not satisfy and that the only important thing in life is to know that our hearts are right with the Lord...it is hard to be so far away from home, but I know it is the Lord's will."[210] This strain was due to the many activities and demands of college as well as married life.

In March 1947, Florence told her family that she had been sick. She felt nauseous and had been fainting.[211] In April, she discovered that she, as well as four other wives in the GI housing unit, was expecting a child. Although the pregnancy made her tired, she soldiered on with her studies. To save money, she bought flannel to make diapers, but since she did not have a sewing machine, she sent fabric home to have her mother make them for her. Jake remained a main draw and was asked to speak at many church services and was out traveling for the church quite a bit, preaching and giving his testimony. Florence found herself alone, pregnant, and getting ready for the baby. She wrote to her mother, "I get a little lonesome here. I keep pretty busy though, and have lots of work to catch up on."[212]

By fall of 1947, Jake was made Assistant Pastor at the church where they both taught. In his free time, Jacob found himself working at the church excavating and digging a new foundation. He also participated in a ministry that reached out to alcoholics living in the Seattle area. Florence was not a big fan of this as she told her sister that she "doesn't like dealing with drunk men and would rather deal with children."[213] Jake continued to be extremely busy as he had at least six services a week. Despite all the work, Florence said Jake was "as sweet as ever" and that she was "pretty lucky to have such a good husband."[214]

As if life could not get busier, Jake and Florence experienced new joy with the birth of a baby boy on October 31, 1947. Jake and Florence named their son Paul Edward. When asked about how he came up with the name, Jake said, "The Paul is after the disciple Paul, and I don't know where the Edward came from."[215] Paul was baptized by his father while visiting the French's and Jacob's families in Oregon over the Christmas holiday.

With this happy addition to the family, the DeShazers struggled financially. Florence supplemented their income by taking care of another child in the morning. Basics like a crib and baby buggy had to be obtained through the generosity of others. Life for Florence was challenging as she spent her day doing homework, housework, and taking care of little Paul. In the meantime, Jake continued to try to balance his schoolwork with two to three speaking engagements every week.

Early in 1947, in preparation of their impending mission to Japan, both Florence and Jacob increased their interaction with Japanese people in the Seattle area. In her letters, Florence noted that "it seems like the Japanese people are eager to hear the gospel and do not rebel against it as so many Americans do."[216] Both Florence and Jake tried to devote as much time as possible to learning Japanese. They also learned to cook Japanese food from a missionary who had just returned from Japan.

Despite their hectic schedules, Jake and Florence found time to cultivate their marriage. The depth of their relationship is portrayed by a poem written by Florence to Jake on Valentine's Day, 1948:

> To My Darling Husband:
> No Good Thing Will He Withhold: Psalm 84:11
> I
> "Come follow me," the Savior whispered,
> "And I will give to you
> Eternal life, and happiness,
> And many earthly joys, too."
> II
> I hearkened to the Savior's voice,
> And listened to His call,
> And now I know the joy and peace
> That comes by giving all.

III
He said, "No good thing will I withhold"
And His words are oh so true.
Because He gave me heaven below
And then He gave me *you*.
IV
Words my dear can never express
What your love has meant to me.
You've been everything and more, dear,
That a husband ought to be.
V
Your kiss has eased each pain I've felt,
Your smile has cheered each day.
Your patient, understanding love
Has helped me in the way.
VI
Your prayers have drawn me nearer to God,
Your faith has strengthened me.
Your daily, constant Christian life
Has been beautiful to see.
VII
And now to make our joy complete
The Lord has sent us little Paul,
To go with us across the sea
In answer to the call.
VIII
My heart is filled with praise, dear,
As I pen these words to you—
"No good thing will I withhold"
I *know* these words are true.[217]

As Jake traveled more in the spring, Florence was left to take care of Paul. When doctors thought he was not gaining enough weight, she told her mother in a letter, "Jake thinks we just weren't feeding him enough so he told me to feed Paul more often."[218] Meanwhile, Florence continued to take care of a neighbor's child, do the housework, shopping, sewing, study her Japanese, and type Jake's term papers since he did not have enough time due to the tasks he was assigned by the church. Florence did not have time to buy an Easter dress; however, Jake helped her when he purchased a blue suit for her. Florence liked it, but thought it was a bit long. However, she told her mother that "Jake likes it that way, though."[219]

In letters home, Florence noted that Jake was always going somewhere. Moreover, Jake was selected by the Mission Board to do deputation work over the summer for the East and Mid-West regions. He was to travel with two field secretaries and while Florence did not like this very much, she was leaving everything in the Lord's hands. In the meantime, Florence stopped watching the neighbor's son because she felt overworked. Jake's speaking engagements were becoming a family affair as Florence and now baby Paul were up with him on the stage as he continued to give his life story.

Finally, in June 1948, both Florence and Jacob received their diplomas from S.P.C. and were recognized in the newspapers. Although they received their diplomas, they did not actually graduate until August when they finally completed all their coursework. Nevertheless, both Jake and Florence received their Bachelor of Arts degrees with a major in Missions. Jake had managed to earn a four-year college degree in three calendar years, just as he had planned. The captions in newspapers and magazines included, "Tokyo Bomber and Wife Get Seattle Pacific Diplomas," "Airman Who Found God," "Doolittle Flyer, Captured, Confined, Devotes Life to Japanese," "Bibles not Bombs," and "Ex-Air Force Man, Wife Will Return to Japan as Missionaries." These followed with stories and photos of Jake, Florence, and young Paul. These news excerpts always noted his connection to the Doolittle raiders, being held as a POW in Japan, and then his conversion. This actually was a good way to get publicity for their upcoming venture, whether they meant to or not.

In the meantime, plans were moving forward for them to depart for Japan to begin their missionary work. But they still had to complete their studies. To help them, Jacob's niece Elaine moved in with them to take care of Paul. By July, they had received word that a house had been found for them in Osaka. Florence wrote to her mother describing the dwelling in the following terms: "It has four rooms…a closet, veranda, doors, electricity, running water, and an inside toilet."[220] This meant two things. First, they would be able to earn an income and hopefully would no longer have to scrape by as they had been doing. Second, and most important, they were close to achieving their dreams of becoming missionaries. In the following weeks, Jake and his family prepared to embark on a great adventure to do the Lord's work in Japan.

Chapter 13

THE JOURNEY TO JAPAN

What then is my reward? Just this: that in preaching the gospel I may offer it free of charge, and so
not make use of my rights in preaching it.
—*1 Corinthians 9:18*

JAKE WAS ORDAINED as a minister in the Free Methodist Church on
August 7, 1948, and could officially be called "the Reverend Jacob
DeShazer." The DeShazer family continued to be busy all the time.
Even little Paul, who normally did not do well at the services, was brought
along. Florence noted that the whole family was tired since they were always coming and going from one place to the next, as well as preparing
for their big move to Japan.

Jake, in addition to other Americans like General McArthur, believed
the Japanese had an insatiable hunger for the Christian Scripture.[221] After
the death and destruction of the Second World War, Jake believed that
the Japanese people would welcome the Christian message of love and
forgiveness. Although Christianity had arrived in Japan via the Jesuits
as early as the fifteenth century, it never took root in the overwhelmingly
Shinto country. The ruling shogun in Japan persecuted the Catholic missionaries, which severely impeded their ability to proselytize.

The devastating war with the U.S. had left many Japanese disillusioned.
Prior to their defeat, Japanese citizens believed that the Japanese homeland was under divine protection by the emperor. But when the emperor
had failed to protect the country, it led many to question the emperor's
status as a deity. Therefore, much soul-searching was underway in Japan
and Jake wanted to be there to offer Christ's message to the Japanese. Also,
communism, exported from Russia, China, and North Korea as a way of
life, was making inroads in Japan. Specifically, the anti-religious philosophy of communism began to permeate throughout Japanese society.

As the time for their departure drew closer, they sold Jake's black Pontiac for nine hundred dollars and received gifts of money and canned food to take on the mission. Their passports arrived with attached visas for their departure to Japan, which would be sometime between November 1, 1948, and January 1, 1949. As the family traveled, Jake spoke at churches every chance he could. His activities and plans were reported in local newspapers as a prelude to their impending mission work. On October 26, 1948, the *St. Louis Post Dispatch* published an article titled "Why God is Calling Me Back to Japan." The story recounted why the Doolittle raider was returning to Japan as a missionary. It was a testimony to Jacob's thinking. The article stated, "The mission will fulfill an ambition DeShazer has nurtured ever since he knelt in a Japanese prison camp beside his dying and emaciated superior officer, Lieutenant Bob Meder. DeShazer said, 'At first, my bitterness against the Japanese seemed more than I could bear. But brooding over poor Bob's death developed my interest in religion and afterlife—in the basic realities of our own existence.'"[222] Jake went on to make the observation that war was not the answer to conflict between nations and men. In his words, "I know now...that love, not hate, is the road to peace among men. That is why Christianity is important...it teaches love."[223] The article also noted the influence that Florence's faith had on Jake. Indeed, Florence's deep personal interest in Christianity strengthened Jake's resolve to return to Japan. The article said that Jake's faith was "all-engrossing" and that he was a "zealous and intense student" of the Bible.[224]

In December, the DeShazer family began making their final preparations for their journey to Japan. Florence noted that she and her husband were "happy to have the privilege of telling the story of Christ to the Japanese."[225] One minor annoyance was that their departure date continued to change. As a result, neither of them were quite sure when they would leave. After many delays, including a maritime strike, the DeShazers finally departed from San Francisco on December 8, 1948, onboard the *U.S.S. General Meigs*. The newspapers came to cover the event as Jake's story continued to be a hot item in the U.S.

Jake boarded the ship six years and eight months after he had boarded another ship, the *U.S.S. Hornet*. On the *Hornet*, Jake was a young man eager for action and adventure. He was also a young man looking to exact revenge against the Japanese for the surprise attack on Pearl Harbor. Jake noted, "This time I was not going [to Japan] as a bombardier, but I was going as a missionary. Now I had love and good intentions toward Japan. How much better it is to go out to conquer evil with the Gospel of peace! We are going to Japan to tell about Jesus and show the way of peace and happiness [to the Japanese]. We hope to see Japan become a Christian nation that Japan may be among the nations that have the joy of worshiping before the true God."[226]

Amidst all the excitement, Jake also recognized that this would not be an easy road for his family to travel. He reiterated that while his "brave little wife was ready for the fight...[t]here might be hardship and trouble, but there would be no turning back."[227] When one stopped and objectively looked at the situation, there was much to fear. Jake and Florence had only a basic grasp of the Japanese language. They were going to a country uncertain about how it would welcome them. Would they be shunned or would they be welcomed? It was hard to tell. Also, how would his child Paul adapt to the life of a missionary family? All these questions must have entered Jake's mind. To find comfort for himself and his family, Jake turned to 2 Chronicles 20:15, "Be not afraid nor dismayed by reason of this great multitude; for the battle is not yours, but God's" (KJV).

The *General Meigs* was not a luxury cruise liner. Each family did not get their own room. Instead, men and women were segregated and stayed in separate cabins. The cabins were packed. Jake's cabin was filled with eighteen men, and Paul and Florence shared a cabin with nine women and four children. With 1,500 passengers on the crowded vessel, personal space was not much of an option. Jake and Florence were also not the only lone missionaries. Other fellow Protestants included a Miss Alice Fensone, a Free Methodist missionary, who was making her first trip to Japan.[228] There were also a fair number of Catholic priests. The Catholic priests remained somewhat of an enigma to Jake. He would often see the priests drinking and smoking cigars with the other men on the boat. This perplexed Jake as he thought that priests had to give up what he believed to be worldly indulgences.

In order to combat the boredom of a two-week journey, Jake and his wife tried to keep themselves busy. They continued to study their Japanese as much as they could. They realized that when they arrived in Japan, there would be a substantial language barrier and the more they studied, the better prepared they could be.

A number of the passengers gave lectures on a variety of subjects.[229] One lecture that appealed to Jake concerned the arrival of Christianity in

Japan. Jake learned that the Portuguese Catholic missionary St. Francis Xavier was responsible for bringing Christianity to Japan in 1549. The Jesuit priest had traveled throughout China, Indonesia, and India and believed that the Japanese were the people most averse to Christianity. Although his work was arduous, he and the Jesuits were instrumental in converting more than a half million people to Christianity in a period of fifty years.

Despite the success of Jesuit and later Franciscan missionaries, the ruling Toyotomi, and later Tokugawa, shogunates did not like the implications of Christianity on their subjects. They believed that a religion that preached truth and freedom in Christ was one that would produce citizens averse to being governed. As a result, the Toyotomis and Tokugawas began to persecute Christians in Japan. The persecution included tactics that Jake had become familiar with. Indeed, Iemitsu Tokugawa, the third Shogun in Tokugawa shogunate, used brutal methods of torture to make Christians denounce their faith. As Mikiso Hane notes, the "most common methods of torture were by water, fire, mutilation, and hanging into a pit headfirst."[230] The climax of the anti-Christian campaign, Jake learned, happened in 1638.

As the Tokugawa shogun tried to squeeze Christianity out of the country, a group of Japanese Christians from the Shimabara peninsula rebelled. The peasant Christians of Shimabara began a general uprising against the daimyo. The Shimbara Christians were led by a sixteen-year-old youth name Amakusa Shiro.[231] Shiro organized the Christians and courted a number of masterless samurai, or *ronin*, to help defend them from the Tokugawa shogun. The Japanese Christians, which now numbered around thirty thousand, traveled to and entrenched themselves in a castle. The Tokugawa shogunate besieged the castle and slowly waited for the inhabitants to starve. After they were weakened, the shogunate attacked the castle with one hundred thousand warriors, massacring virtually everyone.[232]

Shortly after this incident, the shogun expelled all foreigners from Japan. Japan remained in isolation until the arrival of Commodore Matthew Perry in 1854. Perry forced Japan to open itself to foreigners even though there was much internal reluctance to do so. The edict against Christianity that had been established in the seventeenth century was lifted in 1873.

Jake's trip continued to steam ahead toward Japan, stopping for a few days in Honolulu for Christmas. Here Jake and his family were able to visit with the parents of several students they had known as students at S.P.C.[233] Although this was a break from the discomforts of sea travel, the family did not have much time to rest as Jake spoke at a church in Hawaii. After their brief stay in Hawaii, they boarded the ship and left on a Sunday evening. A large crowd gathered and sang gospel hymns when the boat left the harbor.[234]

After numerous days sleeping on an overcrowded boat along with countless bouts of seasickness, they arrived in Yokohama, Japan, on December 29, 1948. Before Jake even set foot in Japan, the Japanese people had been introduced to him through the more than one million tracts concerning the Doolittle raider who had become a missionary that had been distributed throughout the country.[235] The tract contained a space at the bottom for those to sign a pledge indicating that they wanted to become Christians. Up to that point, the publisher of the tract received thousands of signatures. This underscores the reality that Jake believed—the Japanese people were ready and hungry for the gospel. However, commitment required more than just a signature.

Going down the ship's gangplank, the DeShazers were met with a number of reporters and photographers. They had literally just arrived in Japan and already the press was bombarding them. Along with the reporters and photographers were ordinary Japanese citizens who were eager to learn the cause of the change of attitude in a man who had been held as a POW in solitary confinement by the Japanese. They simply could not understand how a heart filled with hatred and animosity could be changed to one that was filled with love for the very people that persecuted him. The intrigued crowd pressed ahead and tried to get a look at Jake. Reporters then began asking him a barrage of questions, "Why are you here? What is the message of Jesus? Do you still resent your captors?" The questions came quickly and Jake, at first, felt a bit helpless. He quickly recounted the highlights of his story, and how he came to Jesus reading a Bible on the floor of his solitary confinement cell. He said that the Lord then enabled him to go to college to obtain an education that would help him become a missionary. Jake told his admirers that the Lord had brought him and his family safely to Japan and that he was looking forward to spreading Christ's message.

The following day, the *Nippon Times* printed a story entitled, "Rev. DeShazer Here to Give Spiritual Help to Japanese." The story included a picture of Florence, Jake, and Paul. In the article Jacob stated, "I have come to Japan to return good for evil. I made a commitment to God…to rescue the people through the love of God."[236] He said that he intended to stay in "Japan all my life." The article recounted details of the Doolittle Raid, how Jake was captured, imprisoned, and how he received a Bible when in jail. Jake said that, in prison, he "learned the barbarity and cruelty of war" and that he believed that "wars should be stopped at once."[237] The article ended by saying that Jake "decided to come to Japan because there were so many war sufferers here."[238] Essentially, he wanted to provide the Japanese with spiritual guidance so that they could come to know Jesus Christ.

As a way to get acquainted with their new surroundings, the DeShazers were taken for a car ride by Colonel Cyril Hill. The colonel drove the DeShazers through several villages and filled them in on what life was like in this part of Japan. In their ride, Jacob and Florence saw the small shops where the Japanese people sold trinkets, handmade dishes, and fruit. The streets were narrow and Florence was concerned about the possibility of running into a small child or a person on a bicycle. The houses were small and did not look as well built as those in America. They noticed that most homes have a small portion of the yard devoted to growing produce and grain. Florence noticed the presence of numerous strips of bamboo poles with strips of paper cut in different shapes. They asked Colonel Hill about this and he said that they were intended to ward off evil spirits. This struck Florence and she said, "Our hearts stirred as we see the superstition and darkness in which people live and we pray that we may soon learn the language so that we can reach their hearts with the gospel."[239]

After the initial wave of excitement, the DeShazer family was confronted with the realities of missionary life. Upon their arrival, the DeShazers were taken to an American style house, but the heating system was not functioning properly, leaving the family damp and cold during the night.[240] For Jake and Florence, the cold was little more than a nuisance, but for little Paul, the chill in the air proved troublesome. Indeed, the next day Paul became sick with a bad cold. By Saturday, Jake and Florence sought out the U.S. Army hospital in order to learn what was wrong with Paul.

The army doctor checked Paul carefully. Although Paul was not gravely ill, the doctor told the family that it was best to leave the baby at the hospital for a week's time. Not only was the hospital warmer, but also Paul would be under the constant supervision of the medical staff. Initially, Florence was opposed to the idea. She did not want to leave her son alone for a single day, let alone one week! In retrospect, this was just one of the many tests of faith that the DeShazers experienced in Japan.

Jake and Florence prayed about the situation and ultimately let Paul stay at the army hospital. As Jake said, "[I]t was good to know Jesus at that time and to realize that He knows all about us and our every problem. When we committed our lives to Jesus, we had given everything. The time of testing had come, but we must not turn back now."[241] Jake then recalled Luke 9:62, which stated that "No man, having put his hand to the plow, and looking back, is fit for the kingdom of God" (KJV). In the end, Jake and Florence left Paul under the care of the doctors and nurses at the army hospital.

Although Paul was sick in the hospital, Jake and Florence continued with their schedule. This included their first visit into the private home of a Japanese woman.[242] Being invited into the home of a Japanese citizen was a big deal. This made a great impression on Florence who noted that when they arrived they did not knock on the door or ring the doorbell, but instead called out *gomen kudasai*, which was a term used when entering a house. When the Japanese woman opened the door, they did not shake hands. Instead, the hostess knelt down and bowed, placing her head on the floor. Before entering the house, the DeShazers took off their shoes and set them aside. Once inside, Florence noticed that the home was sparsely decorated with little or no furniture. Instead of chairs, the DeShazers were welcomed to sit on mats on the floor. They were surprised at how small the house was. According to Florence, the house was barely big enough to stand up. Their hostess then offered them some tea and *omochi*, a gummy substance made from pounded rice wrapped in seaweed. They drank their tea and did the best they could to stomach the appetizer their hostess had given them.

After an agonizing first week, Florence was able to return to the hospital to see Paul. Paul's condition had improved dramatically after the shots of penicillin he was given.[243] On that same Saturday, Jake was busy visiting two churches in Tokyo. At one of the churches, Jake was introduced to Dr. Kaneo Oda. Dr. Oda was native Japanese who had also graduated from Seattle Pacific College. Oda would act as Jake's interpreter when he was speaking in Japan and they would become good friends.

Speaking through a translator was a new experience for Jake. He found that he was becoming more adept at giving his personal testimony.

He had given his story so many times that it had become second nature to him. However, it was difficult when Jake began to preach. During his sermons, he would often have to wait for the interpreter to translate what he said. This sometimes caused Jake to lose his train of thought. On this occasion with Dr. Oda, Jake was overwhelmed with just being able to give his testimony at a Japanese church. Indeed, that day Jake was filled with the Holy Spirit as he said, "We have the sign of prophecy and the resurrection of Jesus Christ from the dead. These are conclusive proofs that the Bible is God's plan of salvation. We cannot save ourselves, but if we receive Jesus, the power needed for salvation will come from heaven and we become the sons of God."[244]

The willingness of the Japanese to hear Jake's message surprised him. The Japanese were definitely curious about this starry-eyed American who had come back to Japan. Indeed, they wanted to know all about him and his family. Perhaps they were perplexed because they were unable to fathom the concept of forgiveness. The Japanese culture places a high value on honor. Honor was a type of pride that manifested itself in oneself, a personal honor, and one's family. If that honor was tarnished or tainted, then it was incumbent on the person who experienced the transgression to right the wrong. In feudal Japan, especially amongst the higher classes and the samurai, this led to blood feuds that lasted for generations in which a cycle of killings was initiated in order to recover the family's honor. An extreme of the honor focus was on display during American encounters with Japanese soldiers in World War II. Rather than be captured by American GIs, Japanese soldiers would often commit suicide to protect their individual and their country's honor.

Perhaps the Japanese listening to Jake were amazed that he was not angry or wanted revenge for the way his honor had been violated in jail. After all, some of the guards had treated Jake less like a human being and more like a wild animal. Here was a man who had been starved, tortured, locked in solitary confinement for months, and given rotten food to eat. Three of his comrades were executed and his other comrades were treated just as poorly as Jake was. If anything, his listeners pondered, Jake should have a heart filled with hatred and vengeance. It became obvious when Jake spoke that his heart had neither hatred nor vengeance. Instead, his heart was overflowing with the love of Christ. Jake preached a message of forgiveness, which was a concept largely foreign to his Japanese counterparts.

Those who heard Jake preach Christ's message of love and forgiveness probably needed additional proof to determine if Jake was sincere. How could one be certain that Jake practiced what he preached? Sure, this sounded good, and, yes, he was here in Japan, but there probably were skeptics in the audience who needed more. If anyone doubted Jake's sincerity, then his actions in January of 1949 would put those claims to rest.

As Jake and his family were leaving for Osaka, they discovered that the judge who had sentenced Jake to life imprisonment was given a death sentence by the Tokyo War Crimes Tribunal. In fact, the judge's father had found Jake and told him the news personally. Jake thought this was unacceptable and worked to get a pardon for the judge. Jake believed this to be revenge, which would not lay the foundation for peace in Japan. Jake used every channel available to him in order to get the judge a pardon, but his efforts were to no avail. The judge's father was heartbroken. However, he appreciated Jake's willingness to try and save the person who had sentenced him to jail. As a gift, the man gave Jake some delicious dried persimmons and *yo-kon*, a sweet Japanese food that the family liked very much.[245] After this gesture, it was hard to doubt Jake's sincerity. He was a genuine person interested in the personal and spiritual well-being of every person he met. His life as a missionary in Japan had just begun.

Chapter 14

DOING THE LORD'S WORK

But thanks be to God, who always leads us in tri-
umphal procession in Christ and through us spreads
everywhere the fragrance of the knowledge of Him.
—*2 Corinthians 2:14*

ON JANUARY 12, 1949, the DeShazers finally received their baggage and their 1948 Black Chevy Sport Coupe. It had taken their
luggage and car a while to arrive, but they were glad when it
did. Upon their arrival, the DeShazers had met a gentleman named Mr.
Yoshiki who arranged for them to live in the upstairs of his home. Mr.
Yoshiki owned a woodworking factory in Osaka and offered to drive more
than three hundred miles to meet the DeShazer's ship when it came in.
Mr. Yoshiki told the family how he wanted to make them as comfortable
as possible in Osaka. Mr. Yoshiki then introduced the DeShazers to the
rest of his family, which included his mother, wife, two sons, two daughters, and his daughter-in-law.[246] There would be no lack of company for
the DeShazers in this house. It is also interesting to note that even though
Mr. Yoshiki was not a Christian, he welcomed a missionary family into
his home as though they were his own family.

While it was a roof over their heads, they had to put a bit of work in
to make this house a home. They had to install their own kitchen, which
included a large oil stove they had brought from the U.S. Mr. Yoshiki
kindly offered to make cupboards for Florence, which she gladly accepted.
A shower was set up downstairs, which was little more than a wooden tub
that used a small electrical device to heat water.[247] All of their sleeping
quarters were in the Japanese style, meaning they had sliding doors and
mats on the floor.

The DeShazers had many things to adjust to in their new home. One
small thing was the noise that the all-wooden sandals make when people

were walking. No matter where they were, they could hear the constant clickity-clack of the wooden sandals.[248] Other more pronounced changes were noticed when they went to the store to buy food and other goods. Some things were cheaper in Japan, such as fried chicken, but it was hard to find beef and soap. Indeed, beef was very expensive and the DeShazers felt as though they would only eat it on special occasions. They were hopeful that they would get a military identification card allowing them to buy rationed goods at the military commissaries and post exchanges.[249]

Driving their black Chevy in Japan proved to be another adventure. Being made in the U.S., the steering wheel was on the opposite side as the Japanese drive on the left side of the road. Additionally, the car was much too large for many of the narrow streets. This caused a few problems. First, the car would often force other motorists off the road, which usually elicited more than one look of consternation. Second, the car could not take the corners of the narrow streets. The family often had to jack up the car and push it over by hand in order to get it around the narrow and sharp corners.

The car not only got the family where it needed to go, it also served as an aid in Jake's ministry. On the top of the car was a loudspeaker that had been rigged to the battery. This created an interesting sight to those living in Osaka. Jake and his family would drive the car and use the loudspeaker to evangelize. Jake got people's attention and as people congregated around the car, Florence, and later his children, would pass out tracts to the interested people. They were also able to advertise the times and location of Bible and Christian education classes they were having at their home.[250]

Within a few weeks, both Jake and Florence became very busy. Jake had created an itinerary of speaking engagements at Osaka's churches. Florence started to conduct Bible studies in the upstairs of the home. Soon, the house became a bustling center of activity, particularly in the evening, as people came to see them. Though they had taken Japanese at S.P.C., it was difficult for the two to converse in this language. To aid them, they found Mr. Nishida who worked as an interpreter for Japanese representatives of the U.S. military police.[251] Mr. Nishida helped Florence and Jake conduct meetings at their home.

One adjustment that the young family had to make to missionary life was the loss of privacy. Just like a doctor, missionaries are perpetually on call. Florence noted, "There is no such thing as privacy here in

Japan. [E]very evening people show up as soon as supper is over...[and] whole families come up with their Bibles and want us to teach them."[252] Although this was a minor inconvenience, Florence and Jake were happy to oblige. They were excited that people were eager to hear the Christian message.

While people showed up in droves to the DeShazer's home, one constant battle was the language barrier. As Florence told it, "It [s]eems impossible that we will ever learn the language, but with God all things are possible."[253] Florence noted that many of the students were eager for the Christian message, but that it took time to figure out how to translate certain concepts into Japanese. Despite this difficulty, they also found some people who spoke English who were simply a joy to teach. Florence recalled one young boy who was proficient in Japanese and English. The young student became a defacto translator for the DeShazers. Florence said that his face would brighten when they read the Bible and that he would tell the others in Japanese what Florence and Jake were trying to convey.[254] Perhaps God had placed this young child in the DeShazer's home for that precise reason.

Within a few months after Jake's arrival in Japan, he had visited and spoken in nearly two hundred different locations. These included churches, factories, schools, people's homes, and public squares. In the meetings, Jake would follow a familiar format. First, he would tell his compelling personal story. He recounted the anger he felt when the Japanese bombed Pearl Harbor and how he wanted a chance to get back at his enemy. After becoming a Doolittle raider and later being captured, Jake learned forgiveness in a tiny prison cell. Next, Jake would introduce the audience to the basic tenets of Christianity. Here, Jake drew on the verse that had been seared in his mind while he was in isolation, Romans 10:9. Jake then told his audience that if they confess that Jesus is Lord and believe in their hearts that God raised Him from the dead, then they would gain eternal life. At that point, Jake would ask the audience members for their decisions. The decision being made by the audience was, basically, one of belief. Did they believe that Jesus was Lord and that God raised Him from the dead? Jake reported, "There has always been a large number who have responded by accepting Jesus as their Savior. Sometimes, at factories, I have seen nearly every worker raise his hand indicating that he has confessed Christ now as his Lord and Savior."[255]

As Jake began to minister in Japan, he touched many people's hearts with the Christian message of love and forgiveness. At the DeShazer home, they began to receive an inordinate amount of mail. Jake believed that this was a sign that his ministry was having an impact on the Japanese. The following is a sample of a letter written by a young lady telling how her life changed after hearing Jake preach:

> On the sixteenth of May I received new life through the message which you gave. Thank you. While you were talking, I cried very much. Through your prisoner-of-war life, you have had a great deal of hatred toward the Japanese people. They were cruel in their treatment of you. I know that you had unreasonable treatment through their ignorance…I have no words to apologize for their rudeness.
>
> However, you have forgiven us, and you came to Japan to save us. I could not help but cry to think of the love which God has put in your heart. Before I was a Christian, I must support my family who are in poor physical condition. I have three brothers and parents, and I had health while they were sick. I worked as a factory girl, but I was discouraged. I tried to kill myself three or four time[s], but without success. I just couldn't go through with suicide. I didn't have any affection toward Japan, and I had little interest.
>
> I always hated God, and I had contracted the sickness of heart beriberi. I quit my work [and] after a week I found a circular of your coming to our town to make a speech. I attended the meeting. And the sixteenth of May will always be a memorable day as well as a revolutionary day for me. By you I was reborn as a child is born on earth. I was now a child born in the heavenly kingdom.
>
> Thank you very much for what you have done. I am full of hope and optimism for the future.[256]

In another case, a young Japanese woman had come to hear Jake speak. She read about Jake in a pamphlet that was distributed in her town. When she saw that Jake was a former Doolittle raider, she decided that she wanted to meet him. She did not want to meet him to ask questions about Christianity, but rather she wanted revenge. The woman's boyfriend had died in the raid of which Jake was a participant. So, she decided that she would go hear Jake speak then would kill him if it were possible.

That day, Jake arrived as usual and began to give his testimony. As Jake recalls, "to her surprise the Spirit of Jesus showed her how wrong her intentions had been. She [became] determined to seek this Spirit of love, which Jesus gives, and God wonderfully helped her. I have seen her many times since that time, and the sweet look on her face is truly convincing of the power of Jesus to change a person's life from hatred to love."[257]

In the spring of 1949, Jake had another wonderful experience at the Office of Strategic Studies (O.S.S.) Theater in Osaka. He was scheduled to talk and his audience was a most interesting one. Indeed, the audience was made up of people who had lost loved ones during the war as well as a large number of former Japanese prison guards. After Jake gave his talk, he began to make his way through the crowd. As he was moving from person to person, he noticed someone in the back. As Jake drew closer, he immediately recognized the face. It belonged to Captain Kudo. The memories of his experience instantly returned to Jake.

Kudo was one of Jake's guards when he was in solitary confinement. He and this guard had been at odds before Jake's conversion. One instance that Jake remembered was when Kudo caught Jake's foot in the cell gate as it was closing. Jake told Kudo to "go jump in the lake" and was seething mad at him. Kudo also witnessed firsthand the change that came over Jake after he had his conversion. Kudo recalled how Jake was a new person when he became a Christian in jail. Jake was calm; his anger had vanished. Instead of exchanging hostile words, Jake would tell the guard *ohayou gozaimasu*, or good morning, in Japanese.

Jake approached Kudo and extended his hand. Jake did not want there to be any hard feelings. When he shook Kudo's hand, Jake gave him a big smile. Kudo then told Jake how he had been reading the Bible for himself. After a brief conversation, Jake was very pleased to hear that Kudo was learning about the Christian message on his own. Jake, being moved by the whole experience, said that both of them had experienced bitter anguish of a terrible war, but now "[w]e see the right thing to do is forgive, to love one another and to work together for one another's happiness."[258]

Later that summer, Jake received important news. He was granted an audience with Prince Takamatsu, the emperor's brother. The meeting would be in Tokyo, which required the family to travel from their home in Osaka. The journey from Osaka to Tokyo was roughly a five-hour trip by car that followed the eastern coastline of Japan. This gave the DeShazers an opportunity to see the exquisite Japanese countryside. Florence, in her letters, took a great interest in her surroundings and talked about the drive at length. On the side of the road, she saw men, women, and children beating their harvested wheat with heavy mallets, sticks, and stones. The people were in such a hurry to harvest the wheat because the rainy season was fast approaching, which meant that they also needed to get their rice crops planted.[259]

As they traveled, it began to pour. The farmers stayed out in the fields as their straw hats and coats kept them dry and allowed them to work. As the rain came down, the farmers hurriedly began to transplant the rice crops into bigger fields that were quickly filling up with water. The people were wading in knee deep and even hip deep in those fields. She saw that some men used a crude ox-drawn plow, while others had a simple hoe to break ground. Seeing this she thought, "I wonder what these people would say if we could transplant them in America for a few days to see the tractors and other farm machinery and big farms."[260] As Florence would later find out, the Japanese farmers were only allowed to own between a one- to two-acre plot of land to grow their crops. This was not a very large area, but to Florence it was surprising just how much they could produce from such a small piece of land.

Once the DeShazers arrived in Tokyo, Jake had his audience with Prince Takamatsu. Accompanying Jake were Colonel Hill and Rev. Kaneda. The three met for nearly two hours. During that time, Jake testified to the prince by retelling his now famous story. After Jake had finished talking, he pressed the prince to see if he could arrange a private meeting with the emperor. This was a bold statement, but one that Jake felt compelled to make. He wanted to share the Christian faith with someone that the Japanese people believed to be a god. Jake perhaps thought that if he could convince the emperor to convert, that it would be a major milestone. The prince politely responded to Jake by saying, "We'll see." Unfortunately, the emperor never did grant Jake a private audience, but Jake continued his work by meeting with as many Japanese as possible.

After Jake's meeting with Prince Takamatsu, he noticed that many missionaries were coming to Japan from China. As he talked to them, he discovered that the communists had kicked out all the Christian missionaries. Jake and Florence saw this crackdown against religious freedom to be a bad sign of something worse to come. This worried Florence who thought that the "communists may try to take Japan sooner than we suppose."[261] Indeed, communists in Japan had already begun holding demonstrations and were now competing with Jake for the attention of the Japanese public. The situation was tenuous. The police had a hard time keeping order when the communists would demonstrate and sometimes the demonstrations would devolve into violence and chaos. In the summer of 1949, demonstrations in large Japanese cities such as Tokyo occurred almost every week.

Thousands of Japanese repatriates returned from Russia and Siberia where they spent time in re-education camps. Those who returned from these camps were well indoctrinated in the communist and Marxist philosophies, which presented a worldview that was anathema to the one that Jake was teaching. Florence sadly noted that many Japanese of all ages were adopting this new ideology. She told the story of one young lady whose parents became communists. This young girl had been coming to Florence's Bible studies and had recently made a commitment to become a Christian. Of course, Florence and Jake were overjoyed. However, one day, the girl arrived at the DeShazer home and told them that her parents refused to allow her to become a Christian.[262] Her parents had become staunch communists and told their daughter that religion acted as an impediment to achieving a perfect society. She was told that religion was an opiate, was used by the bourgeoisie to suppress and oppress the working class. Both Jake and Florence knew that communism, and the militant atheism it espoused, would present a challenge to their message of faith and love. However, they never lost hope in the power of Christ to draw people into the faith.

With communism spreading in the cities and a worsening Japanese economy, Jake began to notice a change in the people who came to hear him speak. Upon Jake's arrival, the central thrust of his message was his conversion to Christianity during his time in prison. The Japanese people were interested in how Jake managed to forgive his enemy. As the summer drew on, questions about Jake's conversion experience lessened. People were more interested in the message of personal salvation. Questions arose such as, "What does it mean to be saved?" "Why does one's soul need saving?" and "How does one become saved?"

Jake and Florence began to notice a disturbing trend. Many of the people who came to hear Jake appeared not to care for their own life. When these people spoke one-on-one with Jake or Florence, some told them that their lives were so hard that they wished they had never been born.[263] Indeed, economic hardships had driven many to the extreme. One young girl Jake met was forced to become a prostitute to feed her family. After doing this for a few months, the girl had a nervous breakdown and tried to kill herself three times. Each time she tried to kill herself, she would think of her family and what would happen to them if she did this. She came to Jake after listening to his message and asked how one becomes saved.

She longed for the hope that salvation brought. Jake spoke with the young woman at length and explained to her what it meant to be saved. This woman is just one of many who yearned for the message of salvation. At that moment, Jake realized that he would begin to focus his preaching more intently on salvation rather than his prison experience.[264] Jake could see that more and more of the people coming to listen wanted him to talk about salvation. They needed to hear about the Christian promise to all those who accept Christ as their Lord.

In this busy time, Jake began to write a book entitled *From Japanese Raider to Japanese Missionary*, in which he recounted his conversion experience and provided a narrative on what Christian salvation meant. Jake spent the summer of 1949 working on the book and it was published in September of that same year. More than ten thousand copies were translated into Japanese and it became popular among the growing Christian population in Japan. As if the DeShazer family could get any busier, Florence and Jake welcomed a new baby boy, John Douglas, on December 11, 1949. Paul now had a baby brother and both Jake and Florence were overjoyed to have the new addition to the family.

With a new baby, Jake and Florence found it extremely difficult to devote time to learning Japanese. The Japanese language had been a stumbling block for Jake and Florence. Jake wanted to be able to rely less on the interpreter so he could more freely speak with the people. While he appreciated the interpreter, he felt as though something was lost in the translation process.

In January of 1950, they began their language classes again. Florence wrote about the difficulty, but that they were making some progress. She concluded that one problem, though, was that baby John was not sleeping through the night. Also, when John began to cry, Paul joined in. Soon, both were crying loudly, which made it impossible for Jake and Florence to sleep at night. [265]

Although Jake was learning Japanese, raising two boys, and preaching, he took up a new cause. In January of 1950, Jake published a small article addressed to General Douglas MacArthur and America's Christian community to stop the execution of forty Japanese war criminals that had been condemned to death. He wanted the U.S. to show mercy despite the atrocities that they committed. Many reporters from Japanese newspapers came to interview Jake. Jake's plea also attracted attention in the U.S., where an article was written on February 11, 1950, in the *Los Angeles Times* entitled, "Ex-Airman Pleads for War Guilty."

Jake wanted the U.S. to demonstrate its Christian virtues by showing clemency to war criminals. Jake implored the Christians of America to "take a strong stand for mercy to be extended to nearly forty condemned Japanese war criminals."[266] He believed that if mercy was shown "a great victory can be won for the cause of Jesus Christ, and also for our country. The people of America know that the war criminals are as guilty as sin and that it can only be through mercy that these men's lives can be spared."[267] As the leading Christian nation in the world, Jake argued, the U.S. "must exercise loving kindness, mercy and righteousness."[268] Jake cited the growth of communism through Soviet expansionism in Eastern Europe as evidence that the world was in dire need of the Christian virtues of faith, hope, and love. Additionally, Jake made the argument that God granted the Allies victory and that victory required that they show their enemies mercy. Executing the war criminals was akin to revenge and, according to Jake, revenge bred revenge, which prevented reconciliation from taking place. Jake urged his fellow Americans to "plea[d] for mercy to General MacArthur and [to] President Truman" in order to save the forty lives.[269]

Unfortunately, his plea for mercy fell upon deaf ears and the war criminals were later executed. This act demonstrated just how sincere Jake was in living the Christian message of love and forgiveness. Jake could have just as easily been tempted to be angry or vengeful toward his captors. However, his hatred had been replaced with love while he was in prison. Jake drew strength from the knowledge that he and Florence's actions were helping the people of Japan. Despite the progress they had made, there was still much work to be done.

Chapter 15

FASTING AND FUCHIDA[270]

May your unfailing love come to me, O LORD,
your salvation according to your promise.
—*Psalm 119:41*

I n 1950, THE world landscape was beginning to change. The lasting
peace that the Allies envisioned after World War II did not last long.
In fact, the clouds of war were brewing over the Korean peninsula. Also, the communist ideology was on the march as it continued to
infiltrate Japan despite U.S. attempts to limit its spread. Jake felt like communism and its hostility toward religion was a threat to his ministry in
Japan. He witnessed firsthand how the communists coaxed the Japanese,
both young and old, into their movement. They promised the Japanese
a sense of purpose and an ideology that would help them make sense of
their hardships. Moreover, it gave them a scapegoat. The communists told
the Japanese people that they suffered because a capitalistic and imperi-
alistic country was ruling them. Ignoring the fact that the U.S. had spent
millions of dollars to rebuild wartorn Japan, they blamed all of society's
ills on the Americans.

Jake witnessed the rise of what he felt to be evil forces that were working against him. It appeared to him that immediate action was imperative
if Japan was to be rescued from communism. He believed that a miracle, or a set of miracles, would be necessary to rebuff communism. Jake
felt that such a miracle could only come about through avid prayer and
fasting.

Following Christ's example, Jake began a forty-day fast. During that
time, he did not withdraw from active evangelistic work like an ascetic
would do, nor did he stop his Japanese lessons. In those forty days, Jake
ate and drank practically nothing. The first three days he went without
food and water. After the advice of his friends, he allowed himself to

drink water, but he strictly followed the fast by eating no food.[271] Jake was not doing this for media attention. Instead, he felt that God was urging him to pray for a spiritual revival in Japan.

Fasting in the Christian community is a spiritual discipline. It is something that one does in order to become closer to God. By denying the body food and drink, one becomes aware of just how reliant human beings are on God. The longer one fasts, the more difficult it is to maintain focus and attention when conducting daily activities like going to work, and spiritual activities like praying. Despite the difficulty, the fasting individual finds that his prayers become more fervent and intense. Jake wanted this kind of prayer because he believed Japan needed it.

Fellow Christians as well as non-Christians were impressed by Jake's fast. One reporter of a leading Japanese newspaper told Jake's colleague, Bob Pierce, of Youth for Christ, that DeShazer's fast had produced a profound effect on the Japanese people.[272] The reporter said that Jake had already won the respect of the Japanese people by his return as a missionary. Now Jake was fasting for them because he truly believed them to be in danger from communism. While the Japanese were accustomed to seeing Buddhist monks fasting, they had never encountered a foreign missionary fasting on their behalf. This produced a great amount of good will toward Jake from the Japanese. While many Japanese did not understand Christianity in the abstract, they liked Jake because he acted as a medium through which the Japanese received the Christian message.

After Jake's fast, he helped to organize a Youth for Christ rally in Osaka. He brought an indefatigable energy to the planning of the event. Not only did Jake pass out thousands of flyers and tracts on the service, he spent many hours in his car announcing the upcoming event. In his broken Japanese, he encouraged the people to come and take part in the event. Jake, feeling that the Lord was going to bring many people to the event, decided to rent a large hall for the service. On the night of the service, Jake could not believe what he was seeing. The hall, which held about three thousand people, was packed.[273] There was barely any room in the hall, and there was an overflow of people outside who strained to hear the loudspeaker. With Jake speaking and Dr. Oda translating, Jake had the sense that this was a momentous occasion. Hundreds of young people came to the altar to accept Christ and be baptized that very evening. Jake was overjoyed with the turnout and felt that his fast had provided some much needed momentum to his ministry. According to the local newspaper, it was the "largest Christian rally that they had ever witnessed."[274]

Another sign that God was listening to Jake's prayers was a meeting between Jake and Mitsuo Fuchida, the lead pilot at Pearl Harbor. Before describing that meeting, it is necessary to examine Fuchida's journey to faith, which is what would bring the two former warriors together in Christian fellowship.

Mitsuo Fuchida was born to Yazo and Shika Fuchida on December 3, 1902. Mitsuo's father, Yazo, grew up in a rural part of Japan, but had ambitions to enter the military academy at Ichigaya, Japan's West Point. Just before enrolling, he lost the sight in his left eye during a baseball game, and with it the chance to be an army officer. Despite this, Yazo never harbored a grudge and instead became a teacher and later principal of the Kammaki Grammar School.[275] Deep down, however, he hoped that one of his sons would have ambitions to be a Japanese military officer.

Through diligence and hard work, Fuchida gained acceptance to Eta Jima, Japan's equivalent of Annapolis. On August 27, 1921, he entered the naval academy at Eta Jima, a small island in the Inland Sea facing Kure Naval Base. His heart was "pounding with great joy," and the sight of the beautiful installation fired his ambition to become an admiral like the great Heihachiro Togo, conqueror of the Russians.[276] Fuchida excelled at Eta Jima, earning high marks in his classes. When he graduated from the academy, he had to decide what field he wanted to go into. During a meeting similar to the U.S. Navy's officer effectiveness reports, Fuchida's commanding officer asked him, "What field would you like to specialize in: gunnery, torpedo, navigation, communications, or submarine?"[277] Absent from that list was aviator.

Fuchida politely responded by saying, "None...I want to be a flyer." A year went by after this meeting, until Captain Kawamura summoned Fuchida into his office. He greeted Fuchida with a smile and said, "Well, Lieutenant, I've heard you're going to be a flyer. That is excellent! Hereafter, able young officers like you should go to the air arm, and airpower should be the main striking force."[278]

Air power would indeed become Japan's striking force. Years later, Fuchida would be selected to be the lead pilot in the Pearl Harbor attack. The Japanese believed that a surprise attack on Pearl Harbor would so devastate the U.S. fleet as to knock them out from a war that, until then, they had been avoiding. On the morning of the attack, Fuchida led a Japanese task force consisting of 353 aircraft in the largest naval air armada ever sent aloft to that date.[279] As the planes raced toward Pearl Harbor, Fuchida had his eyes open trying to assess whether the Americans knew they were coming. When he determined that they had caught their enemy by surprise, Fuchida shouted, *Tora! Tora! Tora!* (Tiger! Tiger! Tiger!), the code word signifying that they had achieved surprise.[280]

The Japanese task force did catch the U.S. by surprise. Fuchida was filled with pride that he and his crew had pulled of such a feat of daring. Years would pass, however, before Fuchida understood that he had left behind more than smashed ships and aircraft and dead and wounded men. He also left behind a nation welded together by the fires he and his men had set—a United States that would not rest until the Japanese had paid in full for their morning's work.[281]

From the zenith of the Pearl Harbor victory, Fuchida would later experience the nadir as American forces began to defeat the Japanese in battle after battle across the Pacific. From the Battle of Leyte Gulf, to Midway, Okinawa, and Iwo Jima, the United States reasserted control in the Pacific and defeated the Japanese. Fuchida was shattered. He believed with his whole heart and soul that Japan's cause had been just. How could Japan's great military have lost to the Americans? This thought consumed Fuchida and he, along with his wife and two children, left to live a simple life in the hills of Nara Prefecture, his native soil.

In Nara Prefecture, Fuchida would become a small farmer. He had saved enough money to purchase a one-acre tract of land from his father-in-law. It was on this farm that Fuchida became consumed by, and worked through, his grief. Being a military man, Fuchida had not the slightest notion of what it took to be a farmer. This did not deter him. He was determined to make a life for his family and believed that hard work and determination would pay off. At night, he poured over books and pamphlets on carpentry, chicken raising, and gardening.[282] Fuchida planted crops and raised chickens and it appeared that his hard work was paying off. Next, he turned his attention to a house for his family.

Fuchida had no practical experience with architecture or carpentry, but he had some good ideas. He had read many books on construction, which told him that the edifice should face fifteen degrees southeast for maximum sun in winter and protection from direct rays in the summer months. Although he had no compass, many times had he stood on the deck of a carrier and used a sextant. One clear evening he took his children Yoshiya and Miyako to the spot where he wished to build. There he gave Yoshiya a long pole and lined him up with the North Star, with Miyako behind him. Using them as a sextant, Fuchida located north and marked off the angle of his home site.[283]

To that point, he had never been spiritual, although by no means was he a pugnacious atheist. He simply accepted the universe of which he was a part without wondering what made it work. Now, as he looked into the bright night sky and saw the North Star, "so steady, so beautiful, and so useful," he began to see the workings of a supreme intelligence. "That night, there on my farm, God began to come into my heart," Fuchida said reverently.[284]

As he continued building and farming, he thought seriously about God's intervention in his war career. "God protected my life during the war," he mused. Why, he wondered. God must have a mission for him, he concluded, although Fuchida could not tell what it would be. But surely whoever created the glory of the skies did nothing without a purpose.[285]

As one season passed into another, from "the miracle of spring" to "the patience of winter," he experienced a revelation, "I began to realize slowly that all things were dependent upon a divine Creator, and that I was living under the grace of God. I could sow seeds; I could plant the saplings; I could draw water with my hands. But they all came from the benevolence of a kind and far-seeing Creator."[286] He became ashamed of his brash confidence in his own abilities and his strict dependence on himself. He began to understand that he, like the plants, lived and grew through the Creator, and that he owed to God whatever abilities he possessed. As he worked on the farm he reflected. The Creator is so wonderful![287]

While Fuchida had begun thinking about God's existence as a result of the passing seasons, he would have two experiences that would push him toward Christianity. The first was in the spring of 1947. In the aftermath of the war crimes trials, Fuchida was determined to find evidence depicting American abuse to Japanese POWs. He would collect the evidence proving his contention and then would attend the next session of the tribunal saying to the judges, "See, this is what you have done. You also have mistreated prisoners. You, too, should be tried."[288]

Fuchida read in the paper that some 150 prisoners of war would be returned to Japan from the U.S. He was determined to visit them and to find out from their own lips just what they had suffered at the hands of the Americans. He traveled to the receiving camp at Uraga Harbor near

Yokosuka, where the released prisoners would disembark from American naval transports. The returning POWs looked weary, sick, and injured, but Fuchida could not tell whether they had been mistreated or abused.

Among the prisoners, he spotted a person who looked familiar. It was Sublieutenant Kazuo Kanegasaki, who had served with him in the Indian Ocean campaign. He was an assistant engineering officer on the carrier *Hiryu*, and everyone believed that he had been killed at the Battle of Midway. He waved to his old friend and said, "Everyone thought you were dead. A tombstone has been erected in your honor in Aoyama Cemetery in Tokyo."[289] Fuchida caught up with Kanegasaki and learned that he had been given to the American authorities by the Swiss.

Fuchida then told Kanegasaki why he had come to Uraga. He told him about the war crimes tribunal and how unfair they had been. He asked his friend if he knew of any Japanese prisoners that were mistreated by the Americans. Kanegasaki said that he had not been mistreated in any way. He then shared a powerful story with Fuchida:[290] Shortly after the end of the war, an American girl about eighteen years old came to the camp as a volunteer social worker. She ministered to the Japanese with tireless energy and kindness. Her name was Margaret Covell. The men called her "Peggy," as did her American friends. She spoke no Japanese, but the prisoners had picked up enough English to communicate with her. "If you are uncomfortable or need anything, let me know," she would say. "I'll do anything I can to help."

With her conscientious care, she touched the prisoners. She also puzzled them. Some three weeks after her first visit, one of the men asked her curiously, "Why are you so kind to us?"

"Because Japanese soldiers killed my parents," she answered.

As the prisoners stared at her in astonishment, she explained that her parents were missionaries who, before the war, had taught at the mission school in Yokohama. Shortly before the outbreak of hostilities, the Covells moved to Manila where they thought they would be safe. When the Japanese captured that city, they fled to Baguio and the mountains of the north. There they remained until the Americans chased the Japanese out of Manila, and it was the latter's turn to flee to the hills. There they discovered the missionaries and found in their possession a small portable radio that they mistook for a secret communication apparatus. They tried the couple as spies, convicted, and beheaded them.[291]

Peggy, who had been living in the United States, did not learn of her parent's fate until the end of the war. At first, she choked with hatred for the Japanese. Then she began to meditate on her parent's selfless service to them. Slowly she became convinced that her parents had forgiven their executioners before death. Could she do less? She volunteered to work with Japanese prisoners of war. Her example of charity and gentleness greatly impressed the men, and they loved her with a pure tenderness.[292]

Fuchida was speechless. "This beautiful story overwhelmed me and made me ashamed," he reflected. He had come to Uraga with hate in his heart. What he found was goodness that he could scarcely comprehend.[293]

The second experience that laid the groundwork for Fuchida's conversion happened in early October 1948 when he saw an American missionary passing out leaflets. He handed one to Fuchida, who glanced at it carelessly before the title caught his attention, *Watakushi Wa Nippon No Horyo Deshita* (I Was a Prisoner of Japan). With the subject of prisoners of war so much on his mind, he read the pamphlet on the spot. The story started with Pearl Harbor and went on to tell how an American sergeant name Jacob DeShazer had become a Christian while in a Japanese prison camp. The pamphlet was only four pages in length, just enough to whet Fuchida's appetite for more.[294]

After boarding a train, he saw among the many advertisements one with the same title as the pamphlet publicizing a book, which DeShazer had written and which was available in Japanese. When Fuchida got off, he found a nearby bookstore and bought the volume. During the next week, he read it cover to cover with amazement.

Fuchida ruminated about the book. This DeShazer had left the U.S. as a soldier who was angry with the Japanese for attacking his homeland. Fuchida could sympathize with that reasoning. However, upon becoming a Christian, DeShazer had undergone a radical transformation. Hate was replaced with love and he wanted to minister to those who had beaten and tortured him.

Fuchida could not believe what he read. The parallel between DeShazer's experience and that of Peggy Covell was not exact, but it was there. This second example of love overcoming hatred hit him with even greater impact. DeShazer had been a tough airman. Fuchida knew the breed well and could identify with him. He then made the decision to read the Bible and to discover what it was all about.[295]

Truthfully, Fuchida had no intention of investigating Christianity as such; he simply wanted to understand DeShazer. In fact, he later conceded that he probably would not have pursued the matter had De-Shazer been just any American prisoner. What secured his interest was DeShazer's being one of the Doolittle raiders. Their exploits had excited his admiration.[296]

Fuchida obtained a Bible and began to read. At Fuchida's first reading, it was the New Testament's moral message that attracted him. The Sermon on the Mount struck a responsive chord. He found the miracles difficult to understand. Nevertheless, he kept reading.

One day early in September 1949, Fuchida came upon the Gospel of St. Luke, chapter 23. For the first time he read the story of the crucifixion. He knew in a vague way that Jesus had been nailed to a cross, but he did not know the details. The Calvary scene pierced Fuchida's spirit. It all came alive in St. Luke's starkly beautiful prose. In the midst of the horror Christ said, "Father, forgive them, for they know not what they do" (Luke 23:24).[297]

Surely these words were the source of the love that DeShazer and Peggy Covell had shown. It came to Fuchida that, as they knelt to die, Peggy's parents had prayed just such words: "Father, forgive them, for they know not what they do." Tears sprang to Fuchida's eyes; he had reached the end of his "long, long wandering."[298]

As Jesus hung there on the cross, He prayed not only for His persecutors, but for all humanity. That meant that He had prayed for Fuchida, a Japanese man living in the twentieth century.[299] By the time he finished St. Luke's Gospel, Fuchida had become a Christian, recognizing Christ as his personal Savior. Since he had no Christian friends, he kept his conversion secret. However, he had found a great joy that imbued him with a new sense of purpose. So he read the Bible in quiet contemplation: "As I labored on the farm I thought of God, creation, the miracles of the season, the growing plants. These things never failed to awe me," he recounted reverently. "And now this new element enriched my life—the knowledge of Christ."[300] Fuchida also thought about the man that he had read about in the tract. He wanted to meet Jake DeShazer, the Doolittle raider turned missionary.

Fuchida asked a friend, Glenn Wagner, chief representative in Japan of the Pocket Testament League, if he could arrange a meeting with De-Shazer. Wagner said this was possible if Fuchida would agree to take part in a grand rally that was to be held in the Central Public Hall in Osaka.

Fuchida agreed. The opportunity to meet DeShazer and talk to his fellow Japanese of his newfound faith in Christ made him excited.

When Fuchida arrived in Osaka, he, Wagner, and an interpreter went to the home where the DeShazers were living. Jake and his family were living with a Japanese family so as to improve his knowledge of the Japanese language, which he spoke only haltingly. It was a high point in the life of each man when the Pearl Harbor commander clasped the hand of the Doolittle raider.[301]

DeShazer told Fuchida that although he had preached all over the country, people were not too interested in his message. He had become quite discouraged. Moreover, he explained how he was dismayed by the situation in Korea, which was on the verge of war, and by the inroads communism seemed to be making in Japan. He decided that a miracle was needed to win Japan for Christ. To this end, he had gone on a strict forty-day fast. During that period, he took no food at all and drank nothing but water.[302]

Thus Fuchida faced a man haggard from fasting and unremitting labor. But DeShazer gave no impression of weakness. His body seemed almost irrelevant, a mere accessory to his dauntless soul. From a thin face, with "something wild" about it, keen blue eyes looked directly into Fuchida's. "His eyes were piercing," Fuchida remembered.[303]

Fuchida greatly admired DeShazer's faith and believed him to be genuine. DeShazer's willingness to fast on behalf of the Japanese people left an indelible impression on Fuchida. DeShazer pointed to Fuchida's conversion as a sign that God had heard his prayers for Japan. Here was a mediator, someone to whom the Japanese would listen and who understood them.[304]

Fuchida and DeShazer talked to one another briefly through the translator Fukuda, and then knelt in prayer together. When Fuchida, Wagner, and Fukuda left, they were filled with God's Spirit and were excited about the upcoming rally. Fuchida could not believe that he would be testifying with DeShazer at the rally.

In the afternoon of the appointed day, the big auditorium was packed. People jammed into the aisles. Outside, more pushed to get in. The crush generated such confusion that the police were asked to help. The rally began with song and the Rev. Ichijiro Saito led the assembly in singing, in Japanese, "What a Friend We Have in Jesus." Fuchida liked this idea, new to him as it was, of singing hymns. "It prepared the people for the Word of God," he said.[305]

Next, DeShazer testified, with Dr. Oda as his interpreter. DeShazer told the crowd of his war and prison experiences, his reading of the Bible, and his remarkable conversion. With his quick smile over his lean face, he declared, "Now I love you as a brother in Christ! Come to know Christ, now, this afternoon!"[306]

The audience listened to Jake intently, and when he finished they gave him a thunderous ovation. Then Saito conducted the group in another hymn, "Washed in the Blood of the Lamb." With this song, the audience grew more anxious. Then Wagner introduced Fuchida. "This is Captain Mitsuo Fuchida, your national hero, who once led the attack on Pearl Harbor. Have you ever heard of him?" Wild applause. "He is not only the hero of the war, he is the hero of the peace. So please listen to his testimony."[307]

Fuchida confidently rose to give his witness in the name of the Lord. He began by sketching out his personal history, starting with his attendance at the naval academy. "Fifteen years passed, and I became one of the aces of the Japanese naval air arm. During this time, I logged thousands of hours of flight time. Then I was chosen to lead the Pearl Harbor attack. I felt very proud to lead this strike as a loyal soldier of my motherland. I did my utmost for my beloved country." Fuchida stopped while the audience roared in its approval.[308]

"But four years later," he continued, "Japan was defeated. In my discouragement, when the war ended, I hated the United States as our former enemy and I hated the war crimes trials. But I want to tell you a beautiful story." Then he talked about Peggy Covell. "Revenge has always been a major motif in Japanese thought," he concluded. "But I am here to say to you that forgiveness is a far greater moral than revenge."[309]

He went on with the story of his own conversion, and how he read DeShazer's tract and then began voraciously reading the Bible. He then appealed to the crowd's war weariness. "I know how you long for peace—personal peace as well as world peace. And real peace comes only through Christ."[310]

When he sat down, he looked over at Jake and there was a huge smile on his face. The audience surged out of their seats and broke into a deafening applause. Jake and Wagner were awestruck. Wagner seized the momentum and invited all who wanted to accept Jesus to come to the front of the auditorium. About five hundred answered the call.[311]

Jake would later remark that giving his testimony alongside Fuchida was one of the high points of his ministry in Japan. Much like Jake, Fuchida took seriously the call to bear witness to the love and healing power of Christ. DeShazer had been instrumental in bringing the light of Christ to Fuchida, so it is fitting that Fuchida would later become an evangelist traveling to the United States to preach the gospel.[312]

Chapter 16

BEING A LIGHT IN A DARK PLACE: THE MISSIONARY WORK OF JAKE DESHAZER

In the same way, let your light shine before men, that they
may see your good deeds and praise your Father in heaven.
—Matthew 5:16

THE DESHAZERS RECEIVED a welcome letter in February of 1950 from the U.S. Government. It told them that all "ex-POWs are to receive a dollar a day for all the time they spent in prison."[313] This was indeed manna from heaven and could not have come at a better time. Jake wanted to buy speakers to take with him to outdoor events and this money would allow him to do this.

As Jake continued his busy travel schedule, he began to notice a pain in his leg. At first he thought it was just a small nuisance, probably due to the long hours he spent standing. As the days passed, Jake began to complain about it. When Florence took a look at the leg, she did not like what she saw. The leg was swollen and the veins looked as though they were popping out. Jake was having trouble putting weight on the leg so he decided to see a doctor.

The doctor told Jake and Florence that his leg needed to be operated on. The procedure was not a serious one, but if left untreated Jake's leg would be in serious trouble. The doctors explained to them that they had to cut the veins and tie them over, which would reduce the leg's swelling and eliminate the pain.[314] Jake thought about it for a moment. The invitations to speak at services were flooding in and Dr. Oda had Jake scheduled for a series of meetings taking place over the weekend. Jake also recently received an invitation to speak in Miyajima, a small mining community located in the Hiroshima Prefecture where the local residents had expressed interest in the Christian message.[315]

Jake saw all of these as opportunities to further the Lord's work. He also did not want to lose the momentum that he had built after the amazing rally with Fuchida. Despite this, he decided that he would have the surgery. After all, he would be no good to anyone if his leg continued to deteriorate.

On March 6, he had surgery on his leg. The doctors cut the leg in five places in order to rearrange the veins and alleviate the swelling. The surgery went well and Jake awoke with a bit of soreness. He was ordered to stay in the hospital for three days in order to recover. Florence was glad for this as she noted that Jake had been working nonstop for weeks. When he was in the hospital, Jake spent some quality time with Paul and little John. He even babysat the two boys when Florence went to teach Sunday school at Nippon Bashi Church.[316] This gave the children some quality time alone with their usually busy father.

As Jake made a full recovery, his travel schedule increased dramatically. Jake seemed to be having meetings or services every night of the week. Jake was so busy each day with visitors and preparing for services that Florence "barely had time to say hello to him. Every day is much the same. Just so crammed full that we can hardly take time to think."[317]

On Easter weekend of 1950, Jake, Florence, and the boys took a six-hour drive to Suyama. Writing to her family, Florence said that Jake would have to preach at a total of eight services on Friday, Saturday, and Sunday. Also, baby John and Mr. Yoshiki's daughter were to be baptized on Good Friday.[318] She relayed that a member of Mr. Yoshiki's family decided to convert to Christianity, which made her happy. This also pleased Jake because the Yoshiki's had been so generous to the DeShazer family, allowing them to live on the second floor of their modest Japanese home.

After Easter, the DeShazers received a pleasant surprise. In a letter sent to them, they discovered that 350 people in Seattle, Washington, had initiated a campaign to raise five thousand dollars to build a new mission home for the DeShazers in Osaka.[319] The announcement came as a complete shock to Jake and Florence. Jake was amazed at the gratitude that these generous people were showing to his family. Jake learned that the house was to be ready in early May and that he and Florence had to begin packing their things. While the new house was being built in Osaka, the DeShazers lived in a rented house in Nishinomiya.

On May 7, 1950, the DeShazer family started putting their belongings into boxes. Until then, they had been living on the top floor of Mr. Yoshiki's house. When the DeShazer family arrived in Japan, their living arrangements took some getting used to. With hundreds of people coming in and out of the house on any given week, it often felt cramped. Sometimes it felt less like a home and more like a train station with people coming and going at all hours of the day.

Despite this, Jake and Florence adapted and soon the second floor became their home. Indeed, much happened on the second floor. It was the site of Jake and Florence's budding ministry. Florence was particularly fond of the many memories she had made as she conducted Bible school with the men, women, and children who attended. Also, Jake and Florence had gotten through to Mr. Yoshiki's daughter who became a Christian just two months earlier. While there was always more work to be done here, the DeShazer's felt as though God was calling them to a new place. They had cast their nets in Osaka, and now it was time to try a different location. Like fisherman, fishers of men cannot stay in one spot forever.

Jake was not able to help much during the packing and moving process. He had been on a strict regimen of fasting and prayer for about forty days, which had left him weak. When he tried to lift a heavy box, he did not have the strength to move it.[320] Luckily, the DeShazers had many volunteers who turned up to help them. The family also had new maids working for them as the other one had been let go because she had tuberculosis (TB). Florence found the process of training the new maids, taking care of two young boys, and getting ready to move challenging. At times, she was tempted "to kick them all out and do the work myself, but that is impossible. I just pray for more patience."[321]

Writing about the rental house to her parents, Florence noted that it was located about halfway between Osaka and Kobe. It was a large, two-story house built in the American style. It had a parlor, a large dining room, and a study that Jake used to prepare his sermons. The maids also had a room on the bottom floor complete with a full bathroom. The kitchen was a bit small and Florence noted that it needed to be expanded at some point in the near future. The upstairs had two large bedrooms and a chapel that the family used for its daily prayers.[322] The chapel was used as a dance hall before it was converted into a religious space.[323] Florence really liked the large garden, as it was a good play area for the kids.

The move to the rental house in Nishinomiya was providential as the large upstairs room of the house was ideal for Sunday school, Bible classes, and church services. In a few months, they had baptized twenty-two people. These people became the nucleus of the now thriving Free Methodist Church in Nishinomiya.

The DeShazers would become well acquainted with the former family. Indeed, the previous owner's daughter-in-law agreed to help teach Japanese to Florence and Jake. Florence noted that the girl was brought up in a Catholic convent and became a Christian. In the convent, she learned English well and acted as an interpreter for Florence.[324]

The DeShazers moved back to Osaka when the new mission house was completed. All in all, the DeShazers liked their new home, and it was not long before Jake began his busy schedule of teaching and preaching. The next big trip for Jake was a two-week excursion to Miyajima where he would spend time talking to a group of coal miners. Jake was thrilled not only to see a new part of Japan, but also to talk to a group of people who had expressed interest in Christianity.

Miyajima was located in part of Japan's most scenic country. The city was on the island of Itsukushima, in the Seto Inland Sea, where it had been a stronghold of Shintoism for centuries. The town was most famous for the Itsukushima Shinto Shrine, which was built in honor of three daughters of the Shinto god *Susano-o no Mikoto*, the brother of the great sun goddess *Amaterasu*.[325]

Historians believe that the shrine was first built in the sixth century. Since then it had been destroyed and rebuilt numerous times, but always in the same location. The shrine itself was located in the sea and was roughly sixteen meters high. It was one of the most sought after views in Japan because during high tide the shrine appears to be floating. Not only would Jake be traveling to one of Japan's most beautiful sights, he would also preach in a town that had been steeped in Shintoism since the sixth century. Jake could not wait to go.

While Florence was excited for Jake's trip to the mines, she was also a bit hesitant about him leaving for such an extended period of time. She knew that he would be gone most of the summer, which meant that she would be left alone with the maids and two young boys. Normally, this would not bother her since Jake was often gone for extended periods of time. In this instance, the sources of her worry were increased crime in the area and the threat of communism.

Her fears were not unfounded. After Jake's departure, Florence and the children were lonesome and a little frightened as there had been seven robberies in the neighborhood within one week's time.[326] She recounted the story of a Quaker missionary friend of theirs who was working with the blind. Apparently, the missionary lived in the home of a prominent town leader who happened to be blind as well. The leader and his daughter became Christians and were now outspoken critics against the communists. These two were trying to galvanize the town residents to reject communism. This put the communist leaders on the defensive and a great enmity developed between the two camps. One night, a young man who was a junior member of the communist party killed the blind man's daughter. Florence's friend, the Quaker, was in the next room and was the first to reach the girl upon hearing her screams.[327] What she saw appalled her.

For Florence, this drove home just how much of a threat communism was. She believed that it was challenging the social order of Japan, which made it, in her view, an evil and corrupting force. She claimed that the Japanese police had increased efforts to root out communists from their society. Florence said that the communists "are always busy circulating literature against the American occupation forces. They are doing their utmost to cause a revolution in Japan. Most of the Japanese people seem to hate communism, but many of the young college students are taken with it."[328] Indeed, there was speculation that many college professors teaching in Japan's elite universities had become communists and were indoctrinating university students to create a populace ripe for a communist revolution similar to the ones nearby in China and Korea. While this frightened Florence, she prayed that God would continue to protect her and her family and give them more time to win "many more souls [for Christ] before the door is closed here in Japan."[329]

While Florence and the kids stayed at home, Jake journeyed southwest to the town of Miyajima where he spent the summer ministering to a group of coal miners. He held two meetings a day with an average attendance of one thousand or more.[330] After each service, there was an opportunity for the miners to ask Jake questions about Christianity. Jake relished this time. Speaking through his translator, he would tell the people about the transformative power of Christ. Many of the miners were interested in the miracles Jake had described in the New Testament. They told Jake that they had never heard of such things. Jake responded by saying that their faith in Christ would help them understand the miracles. He also offered to pray with the people who stayed after the services.

The concerns that were expressed to him for prayer were universal in scope. People prayed for sick or deceased relatives, a better job, a new house, happiness, and relief from the horrors they had witnessed during World War II. Jake was also pleased when many decided to accept Christ and become Christians. Reflecting on the experience, Jake said, "It is a real thrill to tell the gospel message to men who have never heard it before."[331]

The one problem Jake saw clearly was that these Christians would be left on their own. There was no church and no pastors in Miyajima. As a result, the people who became Christians had no guidance. Jake expressed the need for more "Spirit-filled workers" who possessed the theological training and desire to lead the fledgling Christians.[332] To this end, Jake distributed Japanese versions of the New Testament to the miners and prayed that the Holy Spirit would be with these young Christians.

From the mines in Miyajima, Jake reunited with his family and made a trip to Hiroshima, the city where the first atomic bomb was dropped. Jake had heard much about Hiroshima and the horrors suffered by its citizens. He could not imagine the force behind such a weapon. He knew that the bomb caused severe damage to the city, destroying many buildings and killing thousands.

When Jake and his family arrived in Hiroshima, they marveled at how beautiful it was. They were told that the city had been decimated and left in ruins. Five years had passed since the bomb was dropped and the city had made a remarkable comeback. Sections of the city were brand new and it was hard to tell that a few years earlier it had been a little more than rubble.

As they made their way to the British hotel they were staying in, they drove past the building that marked the impact of the bomb when it was dropped. Florence recounts how "our hearts were stirred as we realized the destruction, misery, and death that this bomb had wrought."[333] They learned how all the clocks in the city stopped at 8:15 a.m., the time when the bomb was exploded over the city. Around that building they saw many shadows on the road of structures that had been vaporized. What remained was a photograph of people and places that no longer existed. People had been instantly incinerated.

For Jake, the atomic bomb was symptomatic of a world without

Christ. Humans were fallen beings since they disobeyed God and ate from the Tree of the Knowledge of Good and Evil. Obtaining this knowledge had grave consequences. Since then, mankind had struggled against itself for many centuries. Wars had been fought. However, not until now had a weapon been created that could utterly undo what God Himself had made. Man had achieved such an intimate knowledge of the workings of nature that he could harness that power and weaponize it. Man had discovered a way to literally destroy the world. Jake believed that Christ's message of love and forgiveness was the only way to prevent the use of such a weapon in the future.

Close to this location were many shrines and temples that had been rebuilt. This prompted Florence to observe that "most of the people still know nothing of the saving power of Jesus Christ and that He is able to give them eternal peace."[334] This only confirmed to them the urgent need of their missionary work in Japan.

A few months after their return from Hiroshima, Jake was still busy hitting the streets. He made the decision to confine his ministry to holding evangelistic services in a local building while continuing with the Bible study classes. Florence noted, "nearly every evening finds him out with loudspeakers holding street meetings, passing out literature, and inviting people to services."[335] Indeed, Jake got into a good rhythm with the loudspeakers. He used them effectively to draw people's attention while Florence distributed tracts to the crowd. Unfortunately, the loudspeakers had recently become an issue.

One day, Jake was speaking to the people when a police officer approached the car. Jake asked the officer what the matter was. If it involved a permit to be doing this type of activity, Jake could easily provide the permit he was issued by the Japanese government. The officer responded that the issue had nothing to do with a permit, but with the noise. Evidently, people began issuing complaints that Jake's loudspeakers were making too much noise. When Jake offered to turn the volume of the speakers down, the officer said that it was too late. He would be forbidden to use the speakers inside the city limits. This upset Jake because he had paid good money for the speakers. However, he complied with the officer's wish and discontinued using the speakers. Despite the hindrance, the Lord continued to bless Jake's work.

Shortly after this, Paul became ill. At first, he was not sleeping through the night. He would cry and cry, but no amount of soothing from his parents would calm him down. On Sunday after church services, Paul became sleepy. Jake and Florence thought this was a good sign. They laid Paul down for a nap in the afternoon and he slept through the night. On Monday, Florence noted that Paul had a high fever. They called a Japanese doctor they knew to take a look at their son. The doctor was worried about Paul's high temperature and after an examination determined that Paul had tonsillitis. On Wednesday, Paul shocked his parents as he went into continuous convulsions. Not knowing what was wrong, Jake and Florence took him to the army hospital immediately.[336]

An army doctor confirmed that Paul was suffering from tonsillitis, but also said that Paul had encephalitis as well. As the doctor examined the little boy, Paul went into a post-convulsive coma. Adding to the bad news, Paul's body was unable to regulate his internal temperature. He was now suffering from a 106-degree fever. The doctor told the worried parents that his body temperature had to be cooled or else he might die as he stayed in the coma. The doctor was worried and honestly told the DeShazers that their son's life was in danger.

The nurses at the hospital came into the examining room with several ice packets. They placed theses packets on Paul's body as well as directing an electric fan at him in an attempt to cool his body. At first, this seemed to be working. His body was cooling. Jake and Florence breathed a heavy sigh of relief.[337]

However, a few hours later the situation changed. Little Paul began to shake terribly. After he was put on an IV and oxygen, he continued to be racked with convulsions. At midnight, he almost stopped breathing. The doctor found that Paul's lungs were rapidly filling up with mucous. Paul's life again was in grave danger. As a last resort, the doctor decided to perform a tracheotomy, which would allow Paul to get sufficient oxygen to enter into his lungs. During the operation, the hospital staff suctioned the mucous out of his lungs and then placed him in an oxygen tent. Though he had survived the surgery, his body temperature was extremely high still. The doctors and nurses again packed him with ice to lower the temperature. The situation was extremely tense. The doctor had given Paul a 50 percent chance at surviving the night. The DeShazers prayed that God would protect Paul and help his body recover.[338]

There were times that evening where it looked like Paul would not recover. At one point in the night, Paul gave one nurse quite a scare when it appeared as though he had stopped breathing. The nurse quickly rushed over to Paul's bedside only to find that the little one had started to breath again.[339]

That night, both mom and dad got little rest. They held on to the hope that God would protect their son. God answered the prayers of the parents. Paul did get through the night and stayed in the hospital for a couple of days thereafter. His fever finally broke and went down to 101.

Two weeks after he was rushed to the hospital, Paul was sleeping fine in his own home. The doctor later confessed to Jake and Florence that Paul's recovery was a miracle. The doctor thought that Paul would not survive the night when he was brought in with a fever of 106.[340] Jake and Florence thanked God for providing excellent medical care for their son and seeing them all through this tough time.

Chapter 17

THE JOURNEY HOME

*The church sent them on their way, and as they trav-
eled…they told how the Gentiles had been converted.
This news made all the brothers very glad.*

—Acts 15:3

JAKE CONTINUED HIS rigorous schedule of preaching the gospel and
traveling throughout Japan. Florence summed it up best when, in a
letter to her family, she said, "we are simply swamped with work."[341]
The life of a missionary family was not easy nor for the faint of heart.
Much sacrifice was required, but the DeShazers were happy to do this.
They believed that the Japanese needed to hear the saving message of the
gospel. They experienced the ups and downs that mission work brings.
Jake's journey to the coal miners, for instance, was an amazing experience. He must have felt like Christ's disciple who traveled in uncharted
territory teaching about Christ. To go to a place where Christianity had
never been discussed was a great opportunity. On the other hand, the
persistent question that nagged Jake and Florence was how many of those
people would keep up their newfound Christian faith?

Florence noted that their tent services attracted anywhere from one
hundred to six hundred people. Sometimes, many people would sign the
decision cards. Jake would then pray with the new converts and would
tell them what it meant to be a Christian. They had to live a life of faith,
read the Bible, and attend church. Indeed, Jake noted, "It seems quite easy
to win souls for the Lord, but the number of Christians in Japan does
not increase very fast."[342] The new converts seemed to enjoy Christianity for a while, but then fell by the wayside. Jake attributed this to lack of
churches and trained ministers to ensure that these Christians would be
properly shepherded. Also, Jake mentioned the intense pressure from the
largely Buddhist and Shinto society to not convert to Christianity. The

Buddhist and Shinto priests told the converts that they were abandoning their culture if they became Christians. The conversion story of Mitsuo Fuchida was one such example of the pressures that Japanese Christians experienced.

Upon Mitsuo's conversion to Christianity, his wife did not know how to respond. She was firmly rooted in Buddhism and could not understand why her husband would reject the religion of the Japanese people. Also, Fuchida's fellow military veterans often tried to talk him out of his faith. Christianity was the religion of America, not of the Japanese, they would say. Fuchida was rejecting the faith of his ancestors and was turning to the religion of the conquering and occupying power. For some, this bordered on treason. Needless to say, there were many pressures bombarding Japanese Christians.

Despite the highs and lows of their work, the DeShazers soldiered on. They also welcomed into their family another son, Mark Daniel, born September 21, 1952, and their first daughter, Carol Aiko, born October 10, 1953. Florence was elated to finally have a little girl, although she joked that after having three boys she was better at playing baseball than making curls.[343] During this time, the DeShazers began to talk about a furlough to the U.S. They had been in Japan since 1948 and talking about going home to America was exciting.

The family had noticed that the welcoming attitude of the Japanese from when they first arrived was beginning to change. The curiosity had faded and turned into skepticism. The thought amongst the Japanese public was that the missionaries where there to subvert Japan and to change a culture that had been largely untouched for centuries. Moreover, with war taking place in Korea, the Japanese were frightened that the U.S. would use another atomic weapon. This opened the wounds of Hiroshima and Nagasaki. There arose cries from the Japanese population and intelligentsia accusing the U.S. of war brutality. Gruesome pictures of the bombs' aftermath surfaced and became front-page news. Additionally, the communist party in Japan had continued making inroads with the Japanese public.

On a day trip to Osaka, Jake saw a large number of people waving red flags in a demonstration in the main square by the train station. They had a truck with speakers blaring music and instructions. There were Japanese dressed as Russian communists who were marching three-by-three down the busy street.[344] The police were having a hard time keeping the traffic moving as people would stop and stare at the spectacle. Jake noted that all of this has negatively affected their work because it whipped up strong anti-American sentiment.[345] The DeShazers believed more than ever that they were fighting a spiritual battle against the forces of evil in Japan.

Although Jake and his family were confronted with more challenges than they ever could have imagined, they also experienced moments of joy that gave them encouragement. One such example was the way Jake and Florence acted as go-betweens in Japanese Christian weddings, which the DeShazers were happy to do. The go-between was a combination of parent, best man, and matron of honor. For the Japanese, the engagement announcement was the most important part of a marriage. When a couple approached Jake and Florence with intention to get married, the DeShazers usually counseled the young couple and told them the importance of Christian marriage and how it was a sacramental and spiritual union. Florence, having brought her wedding dress to Japan, allowed young Japanese women to use it since it would be nearly impossible to find a white wedding dress in the American style. On the day of the ceremony, Florence would help dress the bride and stand with them while Jake performed the wedding ceremony. This was quite an experience for both of them as it reminded them of their wedding day.[346]

In January 1955, the DeShazers heard the welcome news that they would be leaving for the U.S. on April 14. Although it would be hard for them to pull up roots and leave after six and a half years, Florence and Jake were excited about their upcoming journey.[347] The children had never met their grandparents, nor did they know the country of their roots. Additionally, they wanted their children to grow up around other children and families rooted in the Christian faith. Jake told his parents that they would leave Japan on the *U.S.S. President Cleveland* and would arrive in San Francisco. Since they would not be able to carry their belongings home, the family sold all their things in Japan. They intended to stay in Salem, Oregon, for a few weeks and then go to Toddville, Iowa. Jake also told his parents of his intention to pursue more schooling at Asbury Theological Seminary in Wilmore, Kentucky.

As their time wound down in Japan, the DeShazers stayed as busy as ever. Florence noted that they had had constant company since Christmas, mainly people wanting to drop in to say good-bye to the family. The parents were also preparing the children for the move. The children, especially Paul, were a bit hesitant about leaving Japan. For him, the home in Japan was all he had ever known. However, Jake and Florence told the children that they would be able to meet their grandparents and would make new friends.

Before the DeShazers boarded the ship bound for the U.S., the Japanese church they helped found held a good-bye party in their honor. It was a wonderful feeling to Jake and Florence as the Japanese Christians expressed their sincere gratitude for all the work they had done. At that moment, Jake began to think about the life he had lived up to that point.

The first time he came to Japan, he was a bombardier. Now he had been living in Japan for more than six years as a missionary who had dedicated himself to preaching Jesus' message of love and forgiveness. Instead of dropping bombs, Jake ministered the message of the Bible. He remembered how perplexed the Japanese were when he first arrived. They asked Jake if he harbored any resentment toward his captors. To their surprise, he did not. He told his new neighbors that Christ's message was love and forgiveness and that he had forgiven those who persecuted and tortured him.[348]

Jake recalled the surreal first months of his stay as he and Dr. Oda went to towns, schools, universities, and public meeting places to preach the gospel. He remembered, "Boy, it was wide open for me. I'd see thousands of decisions for Christ. I'd have them confess with their mouth, 'Jesus is Lord.' And I said, 'Do you believe in your heart God raised Him from the dead?' 'We do,' they answered. They'd put up their hands. Then I'd pray for them and I'd say, 'Now, you pray in Jesus' name.' I said, 'We've got to go on.' We'd have four or five meetings in one day and big crowds. Sometimes we even had ten thousand, and a lot of times there would be one thousand. Seemed like a thousand hands would go up and there were a thousand people there who wanted to be Christian."[349]

Jake cherished those memories, but the time had come to return to the U.S. He said good-bye to the people that he and his wife had come to know and love. In the early morning on April 20, 1955, the DeShazer family boarded the *President Cleveland* and left Japan for America. The trip back home would be long, but Jake and Florence were anxious to see the people they had left behind. They stopped in Honolulu where Jake and Florence managed to hold two services. They were glad to be back on American soil. When people heard of Jake's return, many came up to him and congratulated him on the important work that he and his family had done in Japan.

On May 3, 1955, the *Cleveland* sailed under the Golden Gate Bridge. The DeShazer family could not believe they were in California! After they docked, they caught a sleeper train to Salem, Oregon. The fifteen-hour train ride was a nice reintroduction to the U.S. The route passed through some of the most beautiful countryside in northern California and Oregon. After the trip, they arrived in Salem and took a taxi to Jake's parent's house.

Jake's family was ecstatic to see their son and his family. The grandparents were especially glad to meet the grandchildren whom they had only seen pictures of. Not missing a chance to preach, Jake went to a church rally in Portland. It was amazing how many people turned up to hear him speak. He was still a novelty in the U.S. He attracted Christians and non-Christians alike who were intrigued by Jake's compelling life story. After staying for a few days with his parents, Jake and his family went to visit his brother Glen and his wife, who had a farm in Madras.

Jake thought it was great being back in the town where he grew up. The children also loved the farm as they had a great time riding a donkey and seeing the other farm animals. After staying with Glen for a bit, the family returned to Salem to prepare for their journey to Florence's hometown of Toddville, Iowa.

When in Iowa, the children were able to meet their other grandparents. Jake and the family had little downtime, as they had a full schedule of church meetings.[350] At the church meetings, the DeShazers showed pictures from their time in Japan. This captured the congregation's imagination. Never had they seen pictures of the Japanese countryside. The Japanese, just like many in the congregation, were farmers who diligently tended their fields. While the resentment of the Japanese had subsided significantly since the war's end, some people still harbored ill will toward the Japanese. They were the same folks who listened to Jake with a certain degree of skepticism. Going back to minister to those who tortured you and killed your comrades? Was this love or foolishness? By now, Jake had spoken in front of enough audiences to know that people were thinking these thoughts. He told the church congregants the same story he had been telling for years; a Christian is called to love and forgive their enemies.

Their time in Iowa was spent getting ready for a journey to Kentucky. To get there, Jake and the family needed a car. So Jake looked around the area and settled on a new 1955 Ford Victoria. The '55 Victoria was one of those iconic cars that were used in many movies, usually the ones involving detectives and gangsters. Back then, it was a relatively new model for Ford and was a popular seller in the U.S. It was just what the family needed.

Before leaving Iowa, the family participated in a number of revivals that were happening in the area. They stayed for two weeks as Jake spoke at local churches and outdoor tent meetings. It was over this period that Jake and Florence celebrated their ninth wedding anniversary. Commenting on this, Florence says, "They have been nine wonderful years."[351]

With a new car, the DeShazers packed up and made the two-day drive to Wilmore, Kentucky. The drive took them southeast through Illinois and Indiana. They stayed at two motels along the way before reaching the Kentucky border. Kentucky was different from any place they had ever been. First off, it was hot and humid. The temperatures were in the upper eighties with high humidity that caused perspiration instantly. The De-Shazers also saw the white Southern-style plantation homes that were set back from the road. The homes were huge with large driveways that were shaded with a tree canopy. They marveled at how green the grass was and at the rolling hills that seemed to stretch for miles. On these hills, they noticed beautiful horses roaming leisurely, taking in sun and eating grass. They were intrigued by all the open space because Japan was so crowded.[352]

They arrived on September 1, 1955, and settled into their new home. The house was old and set up strangely, but Florence believed it would be a good place. They had a large bedroom with enough room for a desk so Jake could use it as a study. There was another smaller bedroom for Mark and Carol, and an old utility room, which would be converted into a bedroom for John and Paul. The living room was a good size and would be more than adequate for entertaining guests. Florence was happy about the large kitchen and the space for a nice-sized dinner table. The owners built the family a new garage and they were also in the process of constructing a new bathroom and kitchenette. The location was convenient for Jake as it was only two blocks from the seminary. It was also close to the school that John and Paul would be attending.[353]

Getting settled in their new home would have been easier had their baggage arrived the same day they did. It took the shipping company an extra day to get it to the family. This was problematic for Jake who had to leave on September 2, for a three-week stretch of services and meetings. Luckily for Jake, the crates arrived an hour before he had to leave.

In order to get his things together, he tore off the lids and dumped every-thing in the living room trying desperately to pack. He threw his things in a suitcase, kissed Florence and the kids good-bye, and off he went, leaving Florence to sort out the rest of the belongings that were on the floor. [354]

With Jake gone, Florence was left to get the home in order. The first order of business for her was to buy new slipcovers for the chairs and davenport as the other ones were old and smelled funny. The more closely she inspected the house, the less she liked it. Although her initial im-pression had been favorable, she discovered that the house needed some maintenance. The windows were old and brittle and appeared as though a healthy sneeze could shatter them. Also, the window frames were in des-perate need of a new coat of paint. She took comfort in the fact that the owner of the house had given his word to fix everything up.[355] The family also purchased a portable automatic dishwasher, washer, and dryer from Sears. This made Florence's life much easier and saved her an incredible amount of time. They also bought an upright deep freezer that they placed in the garage. This allowed them to freeze plenty of meat, juice, and fruit. Finally, Jake purchased a typewriter, which would come in handy when he began his seminary studies.[356]

In September 1955, he enrolled in the Master of Divinity (MDiv) pro-gram at Asbury Theological Seminary. The MDiv program was designed for people who had a call for ordained ministry. Jake probably was a bit different from his classmates. Usually, students completed their under-graduate degree in theology and then came to seminary for the MDiv degree and were ordained after they earned their master's degree. Jake was already ordained and had been a full-time missionary for six years. Undoubtedly, he brought a unique perspective to the classroom.

As a first-year MDiv student, Jake was required to take courses that fulfilled his theology requirements. During his first semester, he took classes on Writing a Sermon, the History of the Free Methodist Church, History of Philosophy, and the Teachings of Jesus.[357] Although he had been away from the academic environment for some time, he settled into the routine of his schoolwork. He also met some Japanese students at As-bury and throughout his time there would have them over to his house for dinner. Jake became a good friend of one Japanese student in particular, Jundo Uzaki.

Amazingly, Uzaki's and Jake's paths had crossed before meeting in Kentucky. Uzaki told Jake that he was fifteen years old and was working at the Kawasaki-Kaho factory in Tokyo where he made bomb casings that were used by Japanese planes. That factory was a target during the Doolittle Raid. Uzaki remembered the day of the raid as he and his fellow workers were frightened from the explosions they heard. At one point, Uzaki claims that he could actually see one of the planes passing over the factory. He braced himself for an incoming bomb. However, after the raid was over, the factory was still standing.

When they left the factory they noticed a big crater in the distance. Apparently, a bomb had been dropped from an American plane that fell only five hundred feet from the factory where Uzaki was working. Had the bomb found its target, Uzaki surely would have been killed. Uzaki believed that God had spared him that day for a reason. He later converted to Christianity and believed that he was spared because God was calling him to preach to his Japanese brethren. He then decided to come to the United States to study theology where he found himself in Wilmore, Kentucky. To add another level of intrigue, Uzaki married a 1953 Seattle Pacific College graduate by the name of Miyoko Masada. Uzaki, like Jake, wanted to return to his native Japan to preach the gospel.[358]

As Jake persevered through his studies, the family was getting settled in Kentucky. After a month, the DeShazers, with help from Jake's parents, decided to buy a home. It was much nicer than the home they were currently renting, and they purchased it for a reasonable price.

The three years they spent in Kentucky passed quickly. Jake traveled widely, going to North Carolina, Michigan, New York, and Pennsylvania. During that time, a movie was released on television about Jake called *The Bombardier Goes Back*.[359] The whole family gathered to watch it. It was surreal for Jake to see an actor trying to portray the experiences he had while he was a prisoner in Japan, especially his conversion. No matter how good an actor is, to try to convey that kind of emotion must have been difficult.

Jake graduated with his Master of Divinity degree in June 1958. A few months later, on September 16, 1958, the family was blessed with the birth of Ruth Darlene DeShazer in Lexington, Kentucky. They stayed in Wilmore for a few months after Jake graduated. The mission's board told them that they would be allowed to go back to Nagoya, Japan, for four years. This was the city that Jake and his Doolittle crew bombed many years ago. He was excited about going to Nagoya.

There was much to be done before they left. The house had to be sold, along with all their furniture. Florence was busy ordering the clothing that they would need when they arrived and booking the travel arrangements. This time the trip did not seem as daunting. After all, they had done this before. However, Jake was anxious to get moving as he felt the Holy Spirit calling him back to Japan.

Chapter 18

PIONEER EVANGELISM:
TO AND FROM JAPAN

Submit to God and be at peace with him; in this way
prosperity will come to you. Accept instruction from
his mouth and lay up his words in your heart. If you
return to the Almighty, you will be restored.
—*Job 22:21–23*

ON DECEMBER 31, 1958, the family found themselves bound for
Nagoya, Japan. The Christians in Japan had requested Jake's
help to start a church in the area. Jake felt compelled by God
to return and he believed the theological training he received at Asbury
would help him to convince more people to become Christians. On the
boat, he thought of the many challenges that would present themselves.
What would Japan be like when he returned? Would the people who became Christians still be Christians? Or, had they abandoned their faith?
Jake did not know the answers to these questions. What he did know was
that the peacetime challenges were as big, if not bigger, than those during
the war.[360]

The DeShazers arrived with considerably less fanfare. Hardly anyone was there to greet them, whereas the first time they came there were
hundreds of people eagerly waiting to catch a glimpse of Jake. Jake was
a novelty back then, with reporters from local newspapers pushing and
shoving to get an interview with the Doolittle raider. However, as time
passed, the novelty had faded. The Doolittle raider was just another
Christian missionary. Jake and his family arrived like many travelers do,
anonymously.

They relocated to a place called Smith Town, which was a residential
section built for families of U.S. soldiers during the occupation of Japan.
With the occupation over, many of the U.S. families had left and the

homes were inhabited by Japanese families. Nagoya, then the third largest city in Japan, had no Free Methodist Church, so the DeShazers believed there was much evangelistic potential. As Florence wrote, "It will really be pioneer evangelism."[361]

Soon after arriving, the DeShazers were working. They began having meetings and Bible studies in their home. Florence started Sunday school classes for the children, taught them Bible stories, and had them memorize Bible verses. The children began attending a missionary school, picking up Japanese words and making new friends. The family settled into a familiar routine of travel, preaching, handing out tracts, and trying to engage people about Christianity.

Jake and Florence's daughter, Carol Aiko, recalled what their normal Sunday routine was like during those years. Everyone would wake up early and eat breakfast together around the table. After the meal, Jake would vacuum the floor while Ruth and Carol picked up and did the dishes. Jake would then sit at the table and review the Japanese sermon he had prepared the night before. With the area clean, Paul, John, and Mark would line up all the chairs into a row and turn the table into a pulpit by putting a wooden box on top of the table and covering it with a white table cloth. When they were done transforming the house into a place of worship, the children would leave the house, go into the neighborhood, and bring their Japanese friends to Sunday school.

The children would make their way to the sofa where they would squeeze in to find a space. When all the children had arrived, Florence would teach a Bible story with the felt-o-grams and *kamishibais* (a paper show). Carol remembers how her mother was a master storyteller and that the felt-o-grams and the *kamishibais* made the Bible stories come alive. Next, Florence would go around the room to see if the children had memorized a Bible verse they had been given the week before. If they successfully repeated it for Florence, she gave the child a small pencil as a prize. There were all ages of children there and the older ones would look after and take care that the younger ones could see and hear Florence. Then the adults would arrive and Jake would preach his sermon, pray with them, and sing a few hymns. Carol recalls these memories with fondness, saying, "As a missionary child growing up in Japan, I always felt it was a real privilege to be able to see a church start from the ground level and to watch it grow. I had firsthand experiences of God's work on the mission field—a front row seat! To me, mission work was very much alive and real."[362]

The services held at the DeShazer home yielded a church that took root in Nagoya. Jake then was charged with procuring funds to help build the church. He had to meet with the Free Methodist mission board as well as the Japanese government. With the funds secured and permission to build granted, ground would be broken by early summer 1963. The Free Methodist board also sent a pastor, a single man named Reverend Azuma, to help run the church. Reverend Azuma arrived on April 1, 1963, and was warmly greeted. He was a good preacher and had a wide knowledge of the Bible. Both Florence and Jake hoped that Rev. Azuma was up for the challenge of "pioneer work" in order to get the church established in the community.[363]

The summer passed and due to a number of reasons, construction on the church did not start until late September. When the details to begin construction were finalized, the Japanese Christians of Nagoya had a groundbreaking service. Florence noted that the Japanese made a big deal out of this.[364] The district superintendent came to hold the service. They sang, prayed, read the Bible, and then dug a whole in the ground and buried a Bible with each person scooping a little dirt on it. This carried an important significance. The church was to be built, both figuratively and literally, on God's Word. This was the sure foundation from which the new church would draw its strength.

The DeShazers stayed with the new church a few more months before making plans to return to the U.S. While the church's physical building may not have been finished, Jake was happy with the work Rev. Azuma was doing. He felt comfortable handing him the reigns and was eager to see this church flourish. The DeShazers then left Japan on December 23, 1963, to go back to Oregon for furlough.[365]

The DeShazer family settled into a home they bought in Salem, Oregon. In the spring of 1965, the Free Methodist mission board told the DeShazers they did not have an assignment or home for them in Japan. So, the DeShazers were told to wait. It caused some confusion and questions as to their future for a few years. This was difficult on the DeShazer family and especially on Jacob as he felt that the Lord had called him to minister to Japan!

On Easter Sunday, Florence wrote to her family, "Jake attended the board meeting at the end of March. The board thinks that it costs too much to keep large families in Japan so they want us to stay home for at least four years and then go out when another Free Methodist missionary family comes home on furlough. This means a big adjustment for us as we'll have to take a pastorate or find some other work. We are praying and expecting the Lord to lead us and show us His will."

Jacob still had a love for farming, so in July 1965 they sold their house in Salem and bought a small sheep farm in Gervais, Oregon, where they raised sheep and grew cucumbers. Jacob was returning to his roots. This gave the DeShazer children a chance to learn about their parents' farming skills and also to learn about American schools. A new experience for them was to ride a school bus to school every day instead of taking the train! Jacob continued traveling and speaking in churches and he also took on a part-time job at a food-processing factory.

This pause in their ministry caused Jacob to ponder and reflect on his calling to minister to the Japanese people. It helped him be more determined to get back to Japan as soon as they could to continue the work that God had called them to. Around this time, the Japanese church wrote a letter urging the DeShazers to return to Japan, which prompted the mission board to step up their return process.

In June 1967, the DeShazers leased the family farm and returned to Japan via ocean liner. It had been a three-and-a-half-year furlough for them and they were eager to get back. The extra time in the U.S. had helped to focus their resolve to continue the Lord's work.

This time back in Japan, they were without Paul, who was a sophomore at Seattle Pacific College. As they waved good-bye to him and their ship pulled away from the dock, a few tears were shed, as they knew that they would not be seeing him again for at least five years.

The DeShazers were hoping to move to Tokyo so that their children could attend the mission school there. Unfortunately, no housing was available there and they were stationed in Hitachi where a mission home was already established. For the first time, it meant separation from the children as they had to live in dormitories in Tokyo.

Jake and Florence lived in Hitachi for two years, during which they helped start a new church in nearby Katsuta where Jake helped oversee five churches in that district. After the new church in Katsuta was built, the DeShazers were excited to have their first service there. Jake informed Florence that it was important to take a teakettle for the after-service teatime. That weekend, the DeShazer children came from Tokyo. It was a busy time helping them with their laundry and preparing for their return to school. Jake and Florence had to leave early for the service at the Katsuta Church so they could give the children instructions on how to turn off the heat and lock the doors.

On the way to Katsuta, which was a half hour away from where they were living, Jake said to Florence, "Did you remember to bring the tea kettle?"

"Oh, no!" replied Florence. "In all the hustle and bustle, I forgot all about it!"

"How could you forget such an important thing?" Jake scolded. "Well, I guess we'll just have to stop and buy one."

When they arrived at the Katsuta Church, Florence asked Jake, "Did you bring your sermon?"

He replied, "I've been preaching for twenty years, have I ever forgotten my sermon?" Upon looking in his briefcase, Jake discovered that, indeed, he had forgotten his sermon. There was only one solution. Florence would handle the Sunday school and Jake would drive back home and get his sermon. All the way home, Jake berated himself saying, "How can God use two such stupid and forgetful people?"

Upon arriving home, he opened the door and was met by a blast of heat. The children had mistakenly turned the oil heater on the highest setting instead of off. The wall was smoking and would have burst into flames had Jake not arrived. He burned his hands a little turning it off. He then immediately dropped to his knees and thanked God for sparing the house and all their possessions. Later he told Florence, "God used my forgetter for His good." They were reminded of the Bible verse in Romans 8:28, "In all things God works for the good of those who love him, who have been called according to his purpose."

After two years, a house was built near Tokyo and the family was together again. Four of the children were able to complete their high school education at the Christian Academy of Japan. During this time, John and Mark returned to the U.S. and were drafted into the U.S. Army. Paul was also drafted, but allowed to finish college and enter officer training school.

The new house was built in a suburb of Tokyo called Nishi-Tokorozawa. Land had become very expensive, but as always, the DeShazers wanted to start another church! Again, it meant using their home as a church. The Japanese children would arrive early so that they could find a seat on a large sofa, which they called the Big Chair. Since the children were small, six of them could sit on the edge of the couch and six could squat behind, and six more could sit on top!

In 1972, the DeShazers left for their next furlough. In 1973, Jake received the "Alumnus of the Year Award" from his alma mater. This meant very much to Jake as S.P.C. was the place where he met Florence and where he received his theological training. A local newspaper reported that when Jake heard he had been selected S.P.C. Alumnus of the Year, he remarked they could find someone more deserving.

In 1973, Jake's mother died, having lived to a ripe old age of ninety. Later that year, the DeShazers had to leave Carol Aiko behind for college and returned to Japan accompanied by only one child, Ruth. During this time, the DeShazer children were spread out in five different countries: Paul and Mark in military service, in Guam and Germany, respectively, John in the U.S. after finishing his military service in Vietnam, Carol Aiko in college in Canada, and Ruth living with Jake and Florence in Japan.

Back in Japan and living again in their missionary home in Nishi-Tokorozawa, the DeShazers decided that it was time to build another church. However, since land remained extremely expensive, they got the idea to build a chapel over the carport of their mission house. Using steel beams, a nine-foot by fifty-foot building was erected. It was small but adequate for their small congregation. They had as many as sixty people in the building during their services.

In December 1975, Rex Humbard and his World Wide Ministry came to Japan to do a television special and wanted to include an interview with Jake and Mitsuo Fuchida telling their testimonies together. The program was broadcast all over Japan. Jake and Florence were thankful for yet another opportunity to share the good news. Six months after this event, Fuchida died, in May 1976, and Jake was able to attend his Christian funeral service held in Nara, Japan.

Every week, Jake prepared a sermon in Japanese and Florence led the Sunday school in the newly built chapel. Others helped with the music and teaching. During this time, Carol Aiko had married and she and her new husband, Ken, went to Japan for a year to assist the DeShazers with their missionary work and teach English Bible classes to adults and children. It was hard for the DeShazers to leave this fledgling church, but a younger missionary couple had been appointed to take their place and they knew God's work would continue.

In 1977, Jake and Florence departed from Japan for the last time. They had helped to establish twenty-three churches and led thousands of people to accept the Christian faith.[366] Japan had become their second home.

In a letter written to her family on June 22, 1977, Florence noted, "These are busy but wonderful days here. We have been doing lots of traveling to the different churches for farewell services. It has been encouraging to meet many who were saved during our ministry in the various places. Now some of their children have become Christians and are helping in the church, our grandchildren in the Lord!"[367]

On the DeShazer's last day in Japan, their Japanese friends came from all over and held a farewell party for them. They brought gifts and sang songs, "Blest Be the Tie that Binds" and "God Be With You Till We Meet Again." At the party, Jake spoke about their love for Japan and her people. He then quoted Galatians 5:22–23, "But the fruit of the Spirit is love, joy, peace, patience, kindness, goodness, faithfulness, gentleness and self control. Against such things there is no law." Jake then urged all celebrants present at the party that day to be filled with the Holy Spirit and to pursue God's work vigorously and passionately. Friends said their good-byes and expressed hopes that Jake and Florence would return to their second home again.

As Jake surveyed all that he had done at that point in his life, he thought, "It is marvelous what God has accomplished through a man who dedicated himself [to Christ] in a lonely prison cell."[368]

Chapter 19

THE FINAL JOURNEY: DEATH OF A DOOLITTLE RAIDER AND MISSIONARY

I have fought the good fight, I have finished the race,
I have kept the faith. Now there is in store for me the
crown of righteousness, which the Lord, the righteous Judge, will award to me on that day.
—*2 Timothy 4:7–8*

JAKE RETIRED FROM missionary service in 1978. He and his wife settled back in Salem, Oregon, where Jake was made an assistant pastor at a Free Methodist Church. Jake enjoyed thirty wonderful years of retirement with his wife. During that time, he became a grandfather and great-grandfather. His children, grandchildren, and great-grandchildren were living happy and healthy lives, which greatly pleased Jake and Florence.

As the years moved on, Jake began to suffer from dementia and Parkinson's Disease. The Parkinson's made Jake's hands shake, which made it hard to do simple things like hold a cup or write. The dementia caused him to mix up words, forget names and faces, and to become dependent on others for his day-to-day living. While his body and mind were deteriorating, his spirit remained as vibrant as ever. He was forgetting little things like dates and places, but he always remembered the big picture.

When his pastor at the Salem First Free Methodist Church, Doug Bailey, visited Jake before his death, he asked Jake about his experience as a Japanese prisoner of war. Jake stared back at him, perplexed, and turned to Florence to ask, "Was I a prisoner of war in Japan?" Florence said that indeed he was.[369]

"Oh, I guess I was," was all that Jake could say. However, when Pastor

Bailey asked Jake about his many years as a missionary to Japan, Jake began to talk at length and with great detail. He remembered that he had been a missionary in Japan where he spread the gospel to people who needed to hear Christ's message of love and forgiveness.[370]

On March 15, 2008, at the age of 95, Jake died in his Salem home. Florence and their oldest son, Paul, were there with him when he died. Death was not the end of the journey for Jake, but just the beginning. His life on earth was but a prelude to his everlasting life in the heavenly kingdom.

Jake was buried on March 29, 2008. It was a cloudy day with a cool breeze blowing. Those present were bundled up with jackets, scarves, and gloves. Florence arrived at the base of the gravesite, and was escorted to it by her sons Paul, John, and Mark. The sound of bagpipes and drums led the visitors to the gravesite. At the casket, there were dozens of people gathered, including former Doolittle raider Master Sergeant Ed Horton. Florence sat in a chair in the middle of her family. Also present were members of the McChord Air Force Base Honor Guard, of Tacoma, Washington, who honored Jake with a twenty-one-gun salute. A single bugler then played taps as part of the full military honors that Jake received.[371] Moments later, the crowd gazed to the heavens as a single B-1B bomber from the Thirty-fourth Bomb Squadron flew overhead and disappeared into the clouds. The people present erupted into a cheer as the plane completed its flyover. The Honor Guard members began silently to fold the American flag that had draped Jake's casket. When it was neatly folded, Master Sergeant Douglas Precor presented it to Florence, thanking her for her husband's selfless service to the nation. Friends and family members then took turns laying a single yellow rose on the casket as everyone sang Jake's favorite hymn, "When the Roll Is Called Up Yonder."[372]

A memorial service was held a few hours later at the Salem First Free Methodist Church. At the service, Jake's family members had a chance to speak and share their memories with those present. Paul DeShazer, Jake's firstborn son, read one of his father's favorite passages in the Bible, 1 Corinthians 13:1–13, from the James Moffatt translation, which is the one he would have read in prison. This selection of Scripture explains what love is, "Love is very patient, very kind. Love knows no jealousy; love makes no parade, gives itself no airs, is never rude, never selfish, never irritated, never resentful; love is never glad when others go wrong, love is gladdened by goodness, always slow to expose, always eager to believe the best, always hopeful, always patient. Love never disappears" (1 Cor. 13:4–7, MOFFATT). This passage from 1 Corinthians 13 goes on to enumerate the three great virtues of Christianity: faith, hope, and love. While faith and hope are vitally important to a Christian's life, they cannot exist unless a person is grounded in love.

Jake was a living testament to this passage. He became the epitome of Christian love when he forgave his enemies and decided to become a missionary to Japan. He chose not to repay hate with revenge, but rather to repay hate with love. This is an action that runs contrary to human nature. It is in our human nature to want to repay hurt with hurt, not with forgiveness. Jake demonstrated just how powerful love can be as he forgave those who beat and tortured him.

Later in the memorial service, a video montage was shown that was put together by the co-author of this book and Jacob's daughter, Carol Aiko. It showed pictures of Jacob's life and of him giving his testimony, set to the Christian hymns "Amazing Grace" and "How Great Thou Art." The video ended with the song "There You'll Be" and showed pictures of Grandpa DeShazer with all his grandchildren and great-grandchildren. It then closed with a picture of Jacob kissing Florence on the cheek.

The next to speak were two of Jake's grandchildren, Doug DeShazer and Laura Dixon. Doug wrote a poem honoring his grandfather:

A GRANDSON'S HERO

From a kid in service
Volunteering for a plan
To join a secret mission
That took you to Japan.
The bombs had been dropped
The plane then went down
You were taken captive
Stripped, beaten, and bound.
You gave your life to the Lord
In that prison cell
Made a vow to return
The gospel you would tell.
You lived a life to be admired
One of forgiveness, hope and love

To the world you are a hero
A gift from God above.
Your faith in God proven
In your daily walk with Him
So many words you spoke
Shining light into the dim.
A husband, brother, father,
Grandfather, and friend
Your legacy never forgotten
On that we can depend.
You've left so many memories
Of times we shared together
The times will last in our minds
In our hearts forever.
Playing cards, throwing darts,
Swimming at the lake,
Singing songs in Japanese,
Are all things we will take.
A life of inspiration
Of one that we should live
Thinking only of others
The love of God to give.
This was my Grandpa
I am proud to say
He will be there standing,
Arms open on my day.[373]

Laura talked about how much fun her grandfather was. She recalled how he would give swing rides to the grandchildren on the back porch. She remembered him planting raspberry and blackberry bushes and always letting the kids sneak a few to eat before dinnertime. She also noted how her grandfather kept life simple. It was all about Jesus and love. Those were the two main pillars of his life and they are an inspiration to Jake's children and grandchildren.[374]

The eulogy was delivered by the youngest of Jake's children, Ruth De-Shazer Kutrakun. In the eulogy, she spoke of her father as someone who had felt death's presence before in a Japanese prison cell. His only companion was the Bible, which he read voraciously during the short time he had it. Reading Romans 10:9 changed his life. Hunching over the Bible, he confessed that Jesus was Lord and believed that God raised Him from the dead. He had been saved! Spiritually, he felt like a new person as love entered his being, driving out the hatred that had been dwelling there.

Jake thought, "Lord, take me. I just want to leave this suffering and be with You." At that moment, he noticed his outstretched hands. They were empty, and he thought, "I can't go like this. I've never done anything for the Lord. Just think about it, to appear before the Creator of the universe, after all He's done for me—He sent His Son to suffer and die upon the cross to forgive us our sins. I didn't want to be there for all eternity with empty hands." He became determined to survive the hell he had been living in and devoted his life to Christ and spreading the gospel. He thought, "Lord, I don't want to come to you with empty hands. Give me another chance and I'll try."[375]

As Ruth noted that day, the Lord did give Jake another chance. He survived the prison camp and came home a war hero. He attended Seattle Pacific College where he met Florence. Florence had seen Jake's picture in the paper and was determined to shake the hand of a hero. Little did Florence realize that she would shake his hand—and never let go, not for sixty-one years! Jake and Florence were married, earned their degrees, and moved to Japan, leaving everything behind. He gave thirty years of missionary service to Japan, helping to start twenty-three churches, while being a husband to Florence and raising their five children. Jake could now go to heaven with his hands full.

The benediction was given in Japanese and then in English by Dr. Steve Hattori, a retired pastor in the Japanese Free Methodist Conference. In the emotional benediction, Dr. Hattori noted that Jake had faithfully accomplished the divine commission he was given while he was a prisoner. Here was a man "who put his hand to the plow and never looked back."[376] Hattori praised Jake's many years of missionary service to Japan through which Hattori himself had come to know Christ.

The authors believe it fitting to end a book celebrating the life of Jacob DeShazer with his own words. These lines were printed in the bulletin at Jake's funeral and they best sum up his faith:

I had seen people who could show a beautiful attitude in very trying circumstances, but I did not know
that we can all have this kind of love that is long-
suffering, kind, and patient. However, if we are given
the commandment to love one another, it is surely
possible for us actually to do so. Since God has given
the commandment to love, our part of the transaction
is to put forth an effort and try to have love for others.
This would be a wonderful world if we would all try
to love one another. If we would honestly try and if
we would recognize Jesus as God's Son and our Savior,
God will be pleased with us. I made up my mind to
try.[377]

Epilogue

by Florence DeShazer

J ake and I returned from Japan in July 1977 and had just a week's time to purchase a car, home, and furniture. It was important to us to establish a home where our family could gather because we had not seen some of our children for more than five years.

Then began a very busy schedule of travel and speaking in our supporting church throughout the United States and Canada. We literally lived out of our suitcases, but it was a great opportunity for us to greet old friends and make new ones. We had several long tours of churches in the Ohio area. It became like our second home. One church in Akron, Ohio, built an all-purpose building and named it "The DeShazer House." The pastor and his wife named their son after Jake and the Mayor of Akron declared an official "Jake DeShazer Day" complete with B-25 Mitchell bomber rides.

We officially retired in 1978, but requests continued to come in for Jake to tell his story in churches, veteran's groups, schools, and lots of other places, so for twenty more years we drove more than thirty thousand miles a year traveling and telling Jake's story and of our ministry in Japan.

Being in the U.S. gave Jake and me the opportunity to attend the yearly reunions of the Doolittle raiders. They are a close-knit group and it was great for Jake to see his old buddies and for me to get better acquainted with them and their wives. During these reunions, Jake was usually interviewed by newsmen and given the opportunity to share his story.

In 1993, we traveled to Arlington, Virginia, for General Doolittle's funeral and Jake was asked to pray at his memorial service. General Doolittle was a great leader and was much loved by all the raiders. In 1998, Jake spoke at the Air Force Academy in Colorado Springs and also at the Aerospace facility nearby.

During these years, we returned to Japan three times and were able to visit most of our churches, some of which we had helped start and many where we had ministered. The Japanese Christians welcomed us and treated us royally. Looking at the pictures, some people asked, "Why are all the pictures of you preaching or eating?" Our reply was, "Because that's mostly what we did!"

We have always tried to find time to spend with our family. We have five children: Paul, John, Mark, Carol Aiko, and Ruth. Four of them are married and we now have ten grandchildren and six great-grandchildren.

In 1996, Jake and I celebrated our fiftieth wedding anniversary with most of the family and 150 guests in attendance. Then, in 2002, our family gathered again for Jake's ninetieth birthday celebration. At age ninety, Jake preached his last sermon at a little church on the Oregon coast.

Jake and I lived in an assisted living facility in Salem, Oregon, for three years where Jake passed away on March 15, 2008. I told people at the time of his death that I knew where he had gone and I knew how to get there.

NOTES

CHAPTER 1

1.   C. Hoyt Watson, *The Amazing Story of Sergeant Jacob DeShazer* (Winona Lake, IN: The Light and Life Press, 1950) 22. As mentioned in the Introduction, Watson's book was used primarily for the interviews that he conducted with DeShazer.

2.   Ibid., 19.

3.   Letter from Ruth DeShazer Blackwell to Carol A. Dixon, November 1996.

4.   "Jake and Minto" by Ruth Blackwell and Helen Hindman.

5.   Ibid.

6.   Watson, 20.

7.   Ibid.

8.   U.S. Air Force Oral History Interview with Jacob DeShazer, Office of Air Force History Headquarters, conducted by Dr. James Hasdorff, October 10, 1989, in Salem Oregon, 3. Hereafter this will be referred to as Oral History.

9.   Watson, 23.

CHAPTER 2

10.   Oral History, 5

11.   Watson, 27–28.

12.   Oral History, 7

13.   Watson, 29.

14.   Ibid.

15.   DeShazer interviewed by Watson, 30.

16.   Oral History, 12–13

17.   Letter from Jake to Mother, seventeen days prior to the raid.

18.   Watson, 30.

19.   Ibid.

20.   Ibid., 31.

21.   Ibid., 32.

22.   Ibid.

23.   Ibid., 32.

24.   Ibid., 33.

25.   Ibid., 34.

26.   Ibid., 35.

CHAPTER 3

27.   Oral History, 13.

28.   Watson, 36.

29.   Ibid.

30.   Ibid., 37.

31.   Ibid.

32.   Ibid.

33.   Ibid., 38.

34.   Ibid.

35.   Ibid.

36.   Oral History, 17

37.   Ibid., 39.

38.   Ibid.

39.   Ibid., 40.

40.   Ibid., 41.

41.   Oral History, 15.

42.   Ibid.

43.   Ibid.

44.   Watson, 43.

45.   Ibid., 42.

46.   Oral History, 19.

47.   Watson, 44.

48.   Ibid., 45.

49.   Oral History, 19.

50.   Watson Interview with DeShazer in Watson, 45–47. See also Oral History, 24–25.

51.   Hulda Andrus, "I am the Praying Mother of Jacob DeShazer," *The Bible Meditation League,* April 1957.

52.   John 14:5.

53.   Oral History, 19.

CHAPTER 4

54.   Oral History, 25.

55.   Watson, 47.

56.   Oral History, 25–26.

57.   Oral History, 26.

58.   Watson Interview with DeShazer in Watson, 48.

59.   Oral History, 26,

60.   Watson, 49.

61.   Oral History, 27.

62.   Oral History, 27.

63.   Watson, 51.

CHAPTER 5

64.   Watson, 52.

65.   Ibid., 52–53.

66.   See the Geneva Convention, Part III, Section I, Article 17. It says, "every prisoner of war, when questioned…is bound only to give his surname, first names and rank, date of birth, and army, regimental, personal or serial number."

67.   Oral History, 28.

68.   Ibid.

69.   Watson interview with DeShazer, 54.

70.   Oral History, 30

71.   Letter from Colonel Jimmy Doolittle to Jacob's Mother.

72.   Oral History, 31.

73.   Ibid.

74.   Watson, 55.

75.   Oral History, 34.

76.   Ibid., 35.

77.   Watson, 62.

78.   Ibid., 63.

79.   Ibid.

80.   Ibid., 64.

81.   Ibid., 65.

82.   Ibid.

83.   Watson interview with DeShazer in Watson, 65–66.

84.   Ibid., 67.

85.   Ibid., 68.

86.   Ibid.

87.   Watson interview with DeShazer in Watson, 73.

CHAPTER 6

88.   Watson, 74.

89.   Carroll Glines, *Four Came Home* (Missoula: Pictorial Histories Publishing Company, 1966), 93.

90.   Oral History, 35–36.

91.   Ibid., 36.

92.   Ibid., 36.

93.   Ibid., 37.

94.   Watson, 76.

95.   Watson interview with DeShazer in Watson, 76.

96.   Oral History, 38.

97.   Watson, 77.

98.   Oral History, 40.

99.   Watson interview with DeShazer in Watson, 79.

100. Ibid.

101. Ibid., 80.

102. Ibid., 81.

103. Ibid.

104. Ibid., 82.

CHAPTER 7

105. Genesis 1:1–3.

106. Watson interview with DeShazer in Watson, 87–89.

107. Ibid., 90.

108. Ibid., 91–92.

109. Ibid., 93–94.

110. Ibid., 95.

111. Ibid., 96.

112. Ibid., 97.

113. Ibid., 98.

114. Ibid., 99–100.

115. Oral History, 42.

116. Ibid., 102–104.

CHAPTER 8

117. Watson, 106.

118. Ibid., 106.

119. Watson interview with DeShazer in Watson, 107.

120. Ibid., 108.

121. Ibid., 109.

122. Ibid., 110.

123. Ibid., 110.

124. Ibid., 111.

125. Oral History, 42.

126. Watson, 113.

127. Watson interview with DeShazer in Watson, 113.

128. Ibid., 114.

129. Ibid., 114.

130. Ibid., 115.

CHAPTER 9

131. Watson, 116.

132. Ibid., 116.

133. Oral History, 42.

134. Watson, 117.

135. Ibid.

136. Ibid., 118.

137. Ibid., 119.

138. Ibid., 119–120.

139. Watson, 121. See also Oral History, 48–49.

140. Watson, 121.

141. Ibid., 122.

142. Ibid., 123.

143. Ibid.

144. Ibid.

CHAPTER 10

145. Watson, 124.

146. Ibid., 125.

147. Ibid., 127.

148. Ibid., 128.

149. Oral History, 50.

150. The Service Strip article dated 8 September 1945 was titled "Rescued Tokyo Flyers Get Processing Here," *Service Strip Article*

151. Watson, 130.

152. Oral History, 51.

153. Letter by Jacob DeShazer, Sept 11, 1945.

154. Ibid.

155. Ibid.

156. Ibid.

157. Letter from Perry Wilcox, September 15, 1945.

158. Watson, 132.

159. Ibid.

160. Ibid., 133.

161. Ibid.

162. Ibid., 133–134.

163. Ibid., 135.

164. Oral History, 53.

CHAPTER 11

165. Watson, 137.

166. Ibid.

167. Ibid., 138.

168. Ibid., 139.

169. Ibid., 140.
170. Ibid., 140–141.
171. Ibid., 141.
172. Ibid.
173. Ibid., 143.
174. Ibid., 143.
175. Ibid., 144.

CHAPTER 12

176. Letter from Phyllis in 1996.
177. Watson, 147.
178. Ibid., 148.
179. Ibid.
180. Ibid.
181. Ibid., 150.
182. Ibid.
183. Ibid.
184. Ibid.
185. Ibid., 152.
186. Letter by Florence, 1945.
187. Letter from Florence to Phyllis not dated.
188. Letter from Florence to her Mother, September 1945.
189. Letter from Florence to Phyllis, Fall 1945.
190. Letter from Florence to Mother, October 20, 1945.
191. Letter from Florence to Brother, October 29, 1945.
192. Letter from Florence to Mother, November 15, 1945.
193. Ibid.
194. Letter from Florence to Mother, November 15, 1945.
195. Letter from Florence to Family, December 20, 1945.
196. Letter from Florence to Margaret, January 1, 1946.
197. Letter from Florence to Parents, March 22, 1946.
198. Letter from Florence to Family, March 22, 1946.
199. Letter from Florence to Margaret, April 3, 1946.
200. Ibid.
201. Ibid.
202. Letter from Florence to Family, May 15, 1946.
203. Ibid.
204. Ibid.
205. Letter from Florence to Family, May 25, 1946.
206. Letter from Florence to Family, June 3, 1946.

207. Ibid.

208. Letter from Florence to Mother, June 23, 1946.

209. Letter from Florence to Mother, December 4, 1946.

210. Letter from Florence to Parents, January 24, 1947.

211. Letter from Florence to Mother, March 23, 1947.

212. Letter from Florence to Mother, July 8, 1947.

213. Letter from Florence to Margaret, September 8, 1947.

214. Letter from Florence to Family, September 22, 1947.

215. Watson, 154.

216. Letter from Florence to Parents, January 28, 1948.

217. "To My Darling Husband," a poem written by Florence to Jacob on Valentine's Day, 1948.

218. Letter from Florence to Mother, February 24, 1947.

219. Letter from Florence to Mother, March 30, 1948.

220. Letter from Florence to Mother, July 28, 1948.

CHAPTER 13

221. "A Raider Returns," American Bible Society, September 1948.

222. "God is Calling Me Back to Japan," *St. Louis Dispatch*, October 26, 1948.

223. Ibid.

224. Ibid.

225. Letter from Florence to Parents, December 7, 1948.

226. Watson, 159–160.

227. Ibid., 160.

228. Ibid., 159.

229. Janet and Geoff Benge, *Forgive Your Enemies: Jacob DeShazer,* (Seattle: YWAM Publishing, 2009), 170.

230. Mikiso Hane, *Premodern Japan,* (Boulder: Westview Press, 1991), 127.

231. Ibid.

232. Ibid.

233. Watson, 159.

234. Ibid.

235. Ibid., 161.

236. "Rev. DeShazer Here to Give Spiritual Help to Japanese," Nippon Times, December 29, 1948.

237. Ibid.

238. Ibid.

239. Letter from Florence to Family, December 31, 1948.

240. Watson, 162.

241. Ibid.

242. Letter from Florence to Parents, January 2, 1949.

243. Letter from Florence to Parents, January 1, 1949.

244. Watson, 163.

245. Florence to Margaret, January 1949.

CHAPTER 14

246. He later tells the DeShazers that one of his sons died in the war.

247. Letter from Florence to Glen and Velma, January 12, 1949.

248. Ibid.

249. Ibid.

250. Ibid.

251. Watson, 164.

252. Letter from Florence to Helen, January 23, 1949.

253. Ibid.

254. Ibid.

255. Watson, 165.

256. Letter quoted in Watson, 165–166.

257. Watson interview with Jacob in Watson, 166–167.

258. Ibid., 167.

259. Letter from Florence to Parents, June 29, 1949.

260. Ibid.

261. Letter from Florence to Ruth, July 4, 1949.

262. Ibid.

263. Letter from Jacob to Parents, August 11, 1949.

264. Ibid.

265. Letter from Florence to Parents, January 13, 1950.

266. William Moses, "Ex-Airman Pleads for War Guilty," *Los Angeles Times*, February 11, 1950.

267. Ibid.

268. Ibid.

269. Ibid.

CHAPTER 15

270. Portions of this chapter are taken from Gordon Prange, Donald Goldstein, and Katherine Dillon, *God's Samurai*, (McLean: Brassey's, 1990).

271. Watson, 168.

272. Ibid., 169.

273. Letter from Florence to Parents, February 15, 1950.

274. Ibid.

275. Gordon Prange et al, *God's Samurai*, 1.

276. Ibid., 4.

277. Ibid., 7.

278. Ibid., 7.
279. Ibid., 34.
280. Ibid., 35.
281. Ibid., 37.
282. Ibid., 186.
283. Ibid, 187.
284. Ibid.
285. Ibid.
286. Ibid., 189–190.
287. Ibid., 190.
288. Ibid., 199.
289. Ibid., 200.
290. Ibid., 202.
291. Ibid., 202.
292. Ibid., 203.
293. Ibid.
294. Ibid., 206.
295. Ibid., 207.
296. Ibid., 207–208.
297. Ibid., 209.
298. Ibid.
299. Ibid.
300. Ibid., 210.
301. Ibid., 216.
302. Ibid., 216.
303. Ibid.
304. Ibid.
305. Ibid., 217.
306. Ibid.
307. Ibid.
308. Ibid.
309. Ibid.
310. Ibid.
311. Ibid.
312. Ibid., 282.

CHAPTER 16

313. Letter from Florence to Helen, February 19, 1950.
314. Letter from Florence to Parents, February 26, 1950.
315. Letter from Florence to Parents, February 23, 1950.

316. Letter from Florence to Parents, March 6, 1950.

317. Letter from Florence to Margaret, March 28, 1950.

318. Letter from Florence to Parents, March 17, 1950.

319. "Ex-Doolittle Raider: $5,000 Drive Set for Tokyo Home," *Seattle Times,* 1950.

320. Letter from Florence to Parents, May 7, 1950.

321. Ibid.

322. Ibid.

323. Ibid.

324. Ibid.

325. In Shintoism, Amaterasu is the most important Shinto deity. The Japanese believed that the emperor was a direct descendent of Amaterasu, which made him both God and man.

326. Letter from Florence to Parents, July 3, 1950.

327. Ibid.

328. Letter from Florence to Parents, August 20, 1950.

329. Letter from Florence to Parents, August 12, 1950.

330. Watson, 181.

331. Letter from Jacob to Parents, August 23, 1950.

332. Ibid.

333. Letter from Florence to Parents, October 11, 1950.

334. Ibid.

335. DeShazer Newsletter sent to Family and Friends, Spring 1951.

336. Ibid.

337. Ibid.

338. Ibid.

339. Ibid.

340. Ibid.

CHAPTER 17

341. Letter from Florence to Parents, February 16, 1951.

342. Letter from Jake to Parents, November 6, 1953.

343. Letter from Florence to Parents, September 22, 1952.

344. Letter from Florence to Parents, June 14, 1954.

345. Letter from Florence to Jacob's Parents, May 8, 1954.

346. Letter from Florence to Parents, October 14, 1954.

347. Letter from Florence to Parents, February 13, 1955.

348. Videotape of Jacob DeShazer speaking from home of Mr. Weise, May 7, 1996.

349. Oral History, 60.

350. Letter from Florence, 1955.

351. Letter from Florence to Jacob's Parents, August 29, 1955.

352. Ibid.

353. Ibid.

354. Letter from Florence to Parents, September 1955.

355. Letter from Jacob to Parents, September 30, 1955.

356. Letter from Jacob to Parents, September 30, 1955.

357. Letter from Florence to Parents, October 9, 1955.

358. Uzaki graduated from Asbury Theological Seminary with his MDiv in 1958. He and his wife did return to Japan. However, Uzaki's ministry was tragically short-lived. His wife said that her husband preached only one sermon in Japan before dying of an aggressive cancer. See *Response,* the alumni newsletter of Seattle Pacific University, Volume 26, Number 1, Winter 2003, Footnotes.

359. Letter from Florence to Parents, November 24, 1956.

CHAPTER 18

360. Missionary Tidings, undated article.

361. Letter from Florence to Parents, May 10, 1959.

362. Interview with Carol Aiko DeShazer, August 27, 2005.

363. Letter from Florence to Parents, 1963.

364. Letter from Florence to Parents, October 1, 1963.

365. Ibid.

366. Oral History, 60.

367. Florence letter to Family on June 22, 1977.

368. Jacob DeShazer quoted in Louis Snider, "Missionaries of Love, Farewell," *Missionary Tidings Magazine,* January–February 1978.

CHAPTER 19

369. Doug Bailey recorded on the funeral video of Jacob DeShazer.

370. Ibid.

371. DeShazer Family Scrapbook.

372. Ibid.

373. Ibid.

374. Ibid.

375. Taken from the eulogy given by Ruth DeShazer Kutrakun's, "My Father's Hands." March 29, 2008.

376. Bishop Elmer Parsons speaking about Jacob DeShazer in Lois Snider, "Missionaries of Love, Farewell!" *The Missionary Tidings,* January–February 1978, 15.

377. Insert in the bulletin for Jacob DeShazer's Memorial Service, March 29, 2008.

BIBLIOGRAPHY

Primary and Secondary Sources

Benge, Janet and Geoff. *Forgive Your Enemies: Jacob DeShazer* (Seattle: YWAM Publishing, 2009).

DeShazer Family Newsletter, Spring 1951

DeShazer Family Scrapbook

"Ex-Doolittle Raider: $5,000 drive set for Tokyo home," *Seattle Times, 1950.*

Glines, Carroll. *Four Came Home* (Missoula, MT: Pictorial Histories Publishing Company, 1981).

Hane, Mikiso. *Premodern Japan* (Boulder, CO: Westview Press, 1991).

Letters of Florence and Jacob DeShazer provided to authors by Carol Aiko DeShazer Dixon

Moses, William. "Ex-Airman Pleads for War Guilty," *Los Angeles Times,* February 11, 1950.

Prange, Gordon, Goldstein, Donald, and Dillon, Katherine, *God's Samurai* (McLean, VA: Brassey's, 1990).

Response, the alumni newsletter of Seattle Pacific University, Volume 26, Number 1, Winter 2003, Footnotes

"Rev. DeShazer Here to Give Spiritual Help to Japanese," *Nippon Times,* December 29, 1948.

Snider, Louis. "Missionaries of Love, Farewell," *Missionary Tidings Magazine,* January-February 1978.

Watson, C. Hoyt. *The Amazing Story of Sergeant Jacob DeShazer* (Winona Lake, IN: The Life and Light Press, 1950).

U. S. Air Force Oral History Interview with Rev. Jacob DeShazer, conducted by Dr. James Hasdorff. United States Air Force Historical Research Center, Office of Air Force History, October 10, 1989.

Videotapes

May 7, 1996: At his home, DeShazer tells his story—from Mr. Weise

July 1, 2001: Jacob DeShazer tells his story, Salem, Free Methodist Church Service

1988: Roberts Chapel in Ohio, Florence and Jacob speak.

May 2001: Tokyo Raiders Reunion Banquet, Fresno, California

One Came Back: The Untold Story of Pearl Harbor, Captain Mitsuo Fuchida

April 12, 1987: Coral Ridge Ministries, Dr. James Kennedy talks about DeShazer

2003: Doolittle Raiders Reunion

March 10, 2001: DeShazer speaks at a Prayer Breakfast in Coronado, California

War Stories with Oliver North: Doolittle Raid

The Return of the Bombardier: A True Story of Inspiration

One Hour Over Tokyo: The Doolittle Raid, History Channel

March 29, 2008: Jacob DeShazer's Memorial Service, "Departure for Glory Land," First Free Methodist Church, Salem, Oregon

About the Authors

ONALD M. GOLDSTEIN is Professor Emeritus and former Director of the Graduate School of Public & International Affairs Matthew B. Ridgway Center for International Security Studies at the University of Pittsburgh. A veteran of the Korean War, he is a retired Air Force officer who served for 22 years. He has taught courses in history, public administration, political science, arms control, national security, theory, and practice of international affairs, American foreign policy, international relations and military history.

Dr. Goldstein is the author of more than 60 articles and 22 books including *At Dawn We Slept*, which was runner up for the Pulitzer Prize in 1981 and on the Best Seller List of the *New York Times* for 47 weeks. He won two Peabody Awards for historical work with ABC and was the winner of the National Association of Public Administrators Teacher of the Year as well as the Chancellor's Distinguished Teacher at the University of Pittsburgh. He serves as a consultant for NBC, ABC, CBS, PBS, History Channel, and NHK (Japan). He earned a Bachelor of Arts Degree in History and a Master of Arts Degree in History from the University of Maryland. He also holds Master of Science Degrees in Political Science from Georgetown University and in Public Administration from George Washington University. Goldstein earned his Doctor of Philosophy Degree in History from the University of Denver in 1970. He is married with four children. He and his wife, Mariann, reside in Florida.

✪ ✪ ✪

Carol Aiko DeShazer Dixon is the first daughter of Jacob and Florence DeShazer. She was born in Kobe, Japan, and her middle name *Aiko* means "love-child" in Japanese.

She spent most of her childhood being homeschooled by her mother and attended military and mission schools in Japan. She graduated from Christian Academy in Japan (CAJ) high school. She then attended Aldersgate College in Saskatchewan, Canada, where she received a Bachelor of Arts degree in Christian Education. At Aldersgate, she met and married a Canadian, Ken Dixon, from British Columbia. They were married in

Tokyo by her father on December 19, 1974. The couple spent one year living in Tokyo with the DeShazer's, assisting in their missionary work, teaching English and studying Japanese.

Carol Aiko then attended Spring Arbor College and graduated with a Bachelor of Arts degree in Social Science and Elementary Education. She did her student teaching at Seattle Pacific University, the same school her parents attended. While living in Seattle, Carol and Ken's two children, Laura and Peter, were born.

During the year they were living and working with her parents in Tokyo, Carol Aiko gained a greater appreciation for her parents, their ministry, and all the sacrifices they had made for her and her siblings.

She is very passionate about her parent's legacy and feels strongly that it needs to be told accurately. It is something she wants the world to know more about. She is presently working to make her parent's story more available through documentaries, books, and other media.

Contact the Authors

Dr. Donald M. Goldstein:
DMGPH@aol.com

Carol Aiko Deshazer Dixon:

www.jacobdeshazer.com
or
www.jakedeshazer.com